Labour in Irish History

Bookmarks
London, Chicago and Melbourne

Labour in Irish History

James Connolly

with an introduction by Kieran Allen

Published January 1987
Bookmarks, 265 Seven Sisters Road, London N4 2DE, England
Bookmarks, PO Box 16085, Chicago, Illinois 60616, USA.
Bookmarks, GPO Box 1473N, Melbourne 3001, Australia.
First published in Dublin, 1910

ISBN 0 906224 32 2

Typeset by Kate Macpherson, Clevedon.
Design by Roger Huddle.
Printed by Cox and Wyman Limited, Reading, England.

Contents

James Connolly was born in Edinburgh in 1868. He became a socialist after deserting from the British army when serving in Ireland. After organising the tiny Irish Socialist Republican Party in Dublin he emigrated to the United States, where he became an organiser for the Industrial Workers of the World, the IWW. Returning to Ireland in 1910, he was general secretary of the Irish Transport and General Workers Union during the great Dublin lock-out of 1913. One of the few European socialists to maintain a revolutionary internationalist position against the First World War, he led the Irish Citizens Army in the Easter Rising of 1916. He was executed by a British firing squad on 12 May 1916.

Kieran Allen is a member of the Socialist Workers Movement in Ireland. He is the author of a forthcoming biography of James Connolly.

INTRODUCTION
by Kieran Allen

ON THE MORNING of 12 May 1916 James Connolly was executed by a British firing squad for his participation in the 1916 Easter Rising. The owner of the **Irish Independent**, William Martin Murphy, the man who had led the employers during the great strike of 1913, had campaigned for Connolly's murder.

The execution was to make Connolly a hero of nationalist Ireland. Today the political establishment has named railway stations, hospitals and union meeting halls after him. Almost every shade of opinion, from the dominant Fianna Fail party to Sinn Fein, the political wing of the Republicans, claim Connolly as their political ancestor. Yet his ideas are rarely discussed, still less understood.

The liquidation of Connolly's political ideas began almost immediately after his death. Two months after the Rising, the Irish Congress of Trade Unions met in Sligo. Connolly had participated in many previous congresses as the general secretary of the Irish Transport and General Workers Union. But the congress did not issue a word of protest against his execution. Instead it called for a minute's silence for all those who died during the Rising — *and* for those who had died serving with the British army in the trenches of the First World War. Connolly's own union remained silent on the vital issues of opposition to the war, military repression in Ireland, and the fate of the surviving prisoners from the Rising.

The situation was similar in Britain. Connolly had contributed regularly to **Forward**, the paper of the Independent Labour Party. Yet the paper commented: 'In no way do we approve of the armed rebellion any more than any other form of militarism or war.' George

Lansbury argued that the Rising was 'a crime against the Irish people', while the British Socialist party and the Socialist Labour Party simply damned it as 'foolish'.

Thus the immediate reaction was that Connolly had been a socialist who had strayed into the nationalist camp. On both sides of the Irish Sea the social-democratic tradition drew back in abhorrence.

But this was not to last. Within months of the Rising a tidal wave of nationalism swept Ireland. The repression that followed the Rising, the threat of conscription into the British army, and general war weariness — all contributed. By late 1917 the Archbishop of Dublin was warning: 'The country will shortly be like Russia if our Irish Bolsheviks are allowed to run amok.'

Unfortunately the 'Irish Bolsheviks' were a figment of the bishop's imagination. True, the very same labour leaders who had distanced themselves from Connolly at the Sligo congress were now calling themselves Bolsheviks. But now they were using Connolly's decision to participate in the Rising as an excuse to hide the Red Flag behind the Green. Connolly's 'nationalism' was now invoked to justify giving the leadership of the national struggle to Sinn Fein. In 1918 all Labour candidates were withdrawn from the General Election to make way for Sinn Fein. The future leader of the Irish Free State, Eamonn de Valera, proclaimed that 'Labour must wait' — and the Labour leadership agreed.

Henceforth it was the patriotic James Connolly who made an appearance: an Irishman first, a socialist second. The chains of martyrdom were fixed while his ideas were gagged.

Connolly's tragedy was that he died without leaving an organisation built around his central political beliefs. Despite 20 years of active socialist involvement in Ireland, Britain and the United States; despite countless speeches, articles and pamphlets, Connolly never built an organised party committed to fighting for his principles.

This was not a matter of personal failing. The syndicalist movement to which Connolly was committed belittled political organisation. He himself wrote: 'We believe that the economic organisation can do all that the political party can do and do it much better and with greater safety for the working class.'

But without a party, rival traditions and pressures led to a splintering of Connolly's political ideas. One the one hand there was his record as a trade union militant and his deep hatred of the capitalist system and its exploitation of the working class. On the other hand there was his fight against the British Empire in the struggle for Irish freedom. Two street ballads show the fragmentation of his politics: in one he is the 'hero of the working man'; in the other 'he died a brave son of Ireland'. They make no connection between the two, because after his death Connolly's own politics were buried underneath the twin traditions of social democracy and nationalism.

Labour in Irish History is Connolly's major analysis of the role of the working class in the fight against British imperialism in Ireland. It is indispensible for anyone who wants to recover Connolly's politics, with all its strengths and weaknesses, from the distortions made since his death.

Before discussing the book itself, it is useful to look at the background of the man himself and the conditions under which the book was written.

Despite later valiant nationalist attempts to discover an Irish birthplace for him, James Connolly was born in Edinburgh in 1868. Poverty and unemployment forced him to join the King's Liverpool Regiment of the British army at the age of fourteen — and it was as a soldier of the British crown that he first embarked for Ireland.

The brutality meted out by the British army in Ireland encouraged him to desert, and he returned to Edinburgh to join the socialist movement. After standing unsuccessfully as a candidate for the Scottish Socialist Federation, Connolly found himself blacklisted by the employers. He saw an advertisement for an organiser for the Dublin Socialist Club and took the position in 1896.

Connolly immediately brought some significant changes to the Club. It was renamed the Irish Socialist Republican Party, a change which signals Connolly's commitment to fight on the national question rather than abstain. The new party affiliated to the social-democratic Second International, and soon made contacts with its revolutionary wing. From 1898 onwards the ISRP was distributing literature from the American Socialist Labour Party, which was at the time one of the most left-wing of the parties in the International.

The ISRP was tiny. Its Dublin membership numbered no more than 30. Nevertheless the fledgling party produced a steady stream of propaganda. It published **The Workers' Republic** on a monthly basis; it issued Connolly's first pamphlet, **Erin's Hope: the End and the Means**; and soon the first chapters of **Labour in Irish History** were appearing as articles in **The Workers' Republic**, although it was not to appear in book form until 1910.

The Irish Socialist Republican Party looked to the republican movement as the principal audience for its ideas, seeking to draw republican militants away from the politics of militarism and class alliances. This was a gigantic shift from the general practice of socialist parties at that time, a shift whose scale can be understood only in the context of the Second International of which the ISRP was part.

The Second International had virtually dismissed the prospect for socialist agitation in the colonies then ruled all over the world by the dominant imperialist powers of Europe. It saw the colonial working class as victims of oppression rather than possible agents of change. A leading member of the German Social Democratic Party summed up the general mood: 'We are for the greatest possible protection for the native peoples through the creation of colonial laws protecting their rights.' When they did not lapse into open chauvinism, the social-democratic parties supported limited measures of autonomy. But they believed that this would be achieved through the activities of nationalist parties in the parliament of the colonial country. Thus in Britain the Social Democratic Federation supported the Irish Home Rule Party in its demand for autonomy within the British Empire. Once the national question had been solved through parliamentary reform, said the Second International, the ground would be cleared for the growth of normal social-democratic parties.

Connolly despised this gradualist approach. He represented one of the few socialist parties from the colonies — and found himself on the revolutionary wing of the International. Instead of ceding the fight for Irish freedom to the nationalist forces, he challenged their will to fight against an empire to which they were bound by 'a thousand economic strings'. Instead of looking on the Irish working class as helpless victims destined to wait until after the constitutional questions had been solved, he saw that the fusion of their national oppression and their exploitation as a class might transform them into a powerful revolutionary force. Therefore his argument to all consistent freedom fighters was that they must look to the working class.

We shall return later to the detailed argument that Connolly presented in **Labour in Irish History**. In the 1890s the logic of his position meant that the ISRP attempted to build united campaigns with the republicans. Occasions such as the Boer War, the commemoration of Wolfe Tone's Rising in Ireland in 1798, and the visit of Queen Victoria to Dublin — all provided successful opportunities for joint mobilisation. But the strategy of a republican-socialist alliance was not entirely successful.

The problem was that the centre of gravity of militant republicanism — then as now — veered towards alliances with the more powerful forces of constitutional nationalism, rather than the tiny ISRP. Connolly correctly predicted that efforts to draw the Home Rule Party into campaigns such as that against the Boer War would help only to revive their nationalist credentials in the eyes of the population. Of his experience of united work with republicans, he wrote: 'They will have no exclusiveness, they tell us, and open their ranks to all who would enter, no questions asked . . . As a result, they get what they want — a broad platform. It is so broad that you can never discover where it begins and where it ends.'

The ISRP did not grow. In 1903 it split as the result of a dispute over trade union strategy, and Connolly emigrated to the United States, to join the organisation that he took to be the vanguard of the revolutionary socialist movement — Daniel De Leon's Socialist Labour Party. Unfortunately it was not all that he expected. The party was politically 'hard'; its ideas were 'clear-cut' — but it operated like a sect. When Connolly disagreed on matters concerning religion, the role of the family, or a supposed 'iron law of wages', he was subjected to a witch-hunt within the party. He left in disgust, to become a full-time organiser with the Industrial Workers of the World, the IWW.

It was during the years 1907 to 1910 that Connolly developed a thorough-going syndicalist outlook, based on the belief that the potential of the working class lies in economic, not political, organisation. He wrote the marvellous pamphlet **Socialism made easy** to popularise the politics of syndicalism. His experience of the sectarian behaviour of the SLP had confirmed his antipathy to political organisations. Henceforth he was to see the industrial union, rather than the party, as the motor for change. The party was useful only as an auxiliary wing for contesting elections, he said; the real force was the industrial union.

Connolly returned to Ireland in 1910 to become an organiser for the newly-formed Irish Transport and General Workers Union (ITGWU). Previously he had written a pamphlet for the Irish socialist movement titled **Labour, Nationality and Religion,** to combat attacks on the left by the church establishment. Now he found himself up against the religious question directly — as ITGWU organiser in Belfast at the height of Orange Protestant loyalist reaction to a Home Rule Bill being debated in the British parliament.

Connolly's response to loyalism was crystal clear. He organised loyalist workers into the ITGWU on the basis of militancy in defence of their interests as workers. He sought to forge links between the cross-channel dockers, who were Protestants, and the deep-sea dockers, who were Catholics. He went into the heartland of loyalism in Larne to organise workers in the aluminium plant there. But Connolly never made the slightest concession to loyalism itself. He lambasted the 'gas and water' reformism of Belfast's leading Labour representative, William Walker, *and* his support for the union with England. Although he opposed the class bias of the Home Rule Bill (effectively it would have taken the vote away from much of the Irish working class), he demanded that every socialist take a stance in defence of the right to an Irish parliament. Inevitably the ITGWU lost many of its loyalist members.

The last three years of Connolly's life were momentous. In 1913 he took charge of the ITGWU in the course of the great Dublin lock-out. From the embers of that defeat, he built the first workers' militia — the Irish Citizens Army — to combat the police and strike-breakers.

When the First World War broke out in 1914, Connolly was one of the very few who stuck to socialist opposition to the war. Congress after congress of the Second International had reaffirmed its opposition to war, but in 1914, instead of organising strike action against it in order to bring down the warmongering governments, the parties of the International turned with few exceptions to support those governments, leading their members to slaughter in the trenches. Connolly, on the other hand, began to plan for insurrection in Ireland.

The Irish Citizens Army numbered no more than 200. The workers who had fought so bravely against their employers in the 1913 lock-out had been swept into the mood of chauvinism in the aftermath of their own defeat. To Connolly, the only alternative seemed to be to pressure the republicans into insurrection. From 1915 onwards, he was openly calling on the republican-led Irish Volunteers to carry out an insurrection.

Connolly hoped that the Rising would not only break British rule over Ireland, but would also spark workers' resistance to the horrors of war all over Europe. But Connolly lacked a socialist organisation which could carry through the insurrection, and the republican forces themselves divided on the issue when the day came. Internationally the Rising was premature: a year later it might have tied into the rising wave of opposition to the war which started in Russia and swept Europe. Isolated, it was brutally suppressed.

Paradoxically, **Labour in Irish History** was written as a polemical argument with the 'advanced' Irish nationalist movement — the very people Connolly was to fight and die alongside in 1916.

The Irish nationalist movement prided itself on being an all-class alliance. Both its constitutional and military wings, and even its most left-wing adherents, accepted the need for class unity in the struggle for Irish freedom. The example of James Stephens illustrates this graphically.

Stephens was one of the co-founders of the Fenians in 1858. He devoted his life to organising secret cells of the movement to prepare for insurrection against British rule. He was slandered and despised by the Irish middle class, and reports on the arrests of Fenians show that the movement itself was predominantly working-class, organised among artisans in the towns. Stephens was also a socialist. He joined the First International, organised by Karl Marx. But he considered his socialism a matter of personal preference. Indeed he regarded any attempt to raise social issues within the Fenian movement as the action of a 'Bedlamite' — a lunatic. The need to keep the door open to win Irish men and women from all classes took first place.

The doctrine of 'a union of all classes' was thus all-pervasive. It was reflected in the nationalist interpretation of Irish history, which saw *one* struggle lasting more than 700 years. The nationalist heroes of one generation are replaced by those of the next; the only foil to their bravery being either the apathy of the masses or the intrigues of traitors.

The merit of **Labour in Irish History** is that it tears this image apart. The Jacobite hero, Sarsfield, is shown to be a feudal lord who 'fought not for the freedom of Ireland . . . but rather to secure that the class who then enjoyed the privilege of robbing the Irish people should not be compelled to give way in their turn to a fresh horde of land thieves.' The founder of constitutional nationalism, Henry Grattan, who was credited with winning an independent Irish parliament, is shown to be part of an emerging capitalist class which 'dreaded the people more than they feared the British government'. Connolly argues that Grattan could have used the Irish Volunteers, who had been established while Britain was fighting its American colonists, to win protectionism for Irish industry — but his allegiance with the aristocracy drove him back into the arms of the British garrison.

Connolly reserves his special hatred for Daniel O'Connell. Here was the nationalist counter-revolutionary spirit personified: Catholic emancipation was to precede even the constitutional agitation for independence. The detail that Connolly produces on O'Connell's relationship with the trade unions is shocking even by today's standards.

He treats the more militant successors to O'Connell, the Young Irelanders, with contempt. The pale shadow of the Europe-wide revolutionary movement of 1848 produced more poets than fighters. Their problem was that 'they were as rabidly solicitous about the rights of the landlord as were the chiefs of the English government.' And this was in the midst of the Great Famine.

Connolly's aim, however, is not to catalogue a tale of horrors. It is to use historical evidence in order to convince the most militant nationalists that a 'union of classes' leads to disaster. Central to Connolly's argument is the cowardice of the Irish bourgeoisie. With the exception of the revolutionary period between 1798 and 1803, their record has been one of appalling betrayal. Even at this high point many of their number did not back Wolfe Tone's United Irishmen, joining instead the Catholic-led militia in order to oppose them.

To what can we attribute this cowardice of the Irish bourgeoisie in fighting for their own interests? Connolly argues that the lack of natural resources in Ireland made Irish manufacture weak. To survive against rival English industry it would have needed a stringent system of protection — and that in turn would only be won by a complete break with the landed aristocracy and all others who depended on the British garrison to protect them from 'the natives'. Thus harsher economic conditions demanded that, to survive and develop as a class, the bourgeoisie would have to take more drastic measures in Ireland than it did elsewhere. Its own weakness, says Connolly, meant that it lacked the political will to take those revolutionary measures.

Here is how Connolly describes the full integration of Ireland into the British Empire in 1800: 'The Act of Union was made possible because Irish manufacture was weak and consequently had not an energetic capitalist class with sufficient public spirit and influence to prevent the union.' This view was the exact reverse of that held by nationalist politicians and historians. The Home Rule Party claimed that it was the lack of a native parliament which *caused* the weakness of Irish manufacture, and that, conversely, home rule would bring a revival of native capitalism.

Connolly viewed this 'parliamentarian view' of Irish history as especially dangerous, holding out as it did the idea that there was a capitalist solution to the Irish struggle. In an earlier pamphlet, **Erin's Hope**, he went to considerable length to attack this idea, arguing that home rule would not compensate for lack of capital or resources. Moreover, on a world scale, capitalism had already glutted the limited markets available: 'The thoughtful Irish patriot will throw rant aside and freely recognise that it is impossible for Ireland to do what those other countries cannot do, with their greater advantages, viz. to attain prosperity by establishing a manufacturing system in a world market already glutted with every conceivable kind of commodity . . . Our chance of making Ireland a manufacturing country depends on us becoming the worst blacklegs in Europe.'

Connolly was absolutely correct in predicting that native Irish capitalism would exact tremendous sacrifices from its workers. He was also correct in believing that an independent parliament could not escape the trends of the world economy. But his concept of a 'limited market', and hence the *impossibility* of Irish capitalist development, meant that he was to ignore the opportunities that 20th-century republicanism was to offer capitalism. Connolly, for example, never seriously challenged the economic ideas of Sinn Fein's founder, Arthur Griffith, even when the latter spelt out how Irish capitalism could revive. Connolly continued to regard Griffith's views on the subject as virtually irrelevant, arguing that the *logic* of the struggle for Irish independence led to an assault on capitalism itself.

Instead Connolly concentrated his fire on the older Home Rule tradition of constitutional nationalism. He believed that if republicans were to break fully with this tradition, there was nothing to stop them moving leftwards into the socialist camp. The result is a surprising gap in Connolly's writings: on the politics of republicanism itself, which was being reborn in the cities of Ireland alongside the labour movement.

This blind spot of Connolly's is reflected in **Labour in Irish History**. While he makes a clear materialist analysis of the likes of O'Connell, Grattan and the Young Irelanders, this is not the case with the forerunners of the more militant republican tradition. The United Irishmen, for instance, are presented simply as a movement of the Catholic and Protestant poor, brought together by 'the activity of a revolutionist' (Wolfe Tone) and 'a great dramatic event' (the French revolution). The patriotic shift amongst the capitalist class at the time is seen as merely coincidental.

Yet the United Irishmen were firmly led by the most radical element of the Irish capitalist class. Tone's famous and ambiguous appeal to the 'men of no property' was by way of a threat to the more moderate members of his own class. A brief pen picture of the leadership of the United Irishmen illustrates the point clearly:

> In the North there was Robert Simms, merchant and part-owner of a newspaper; Thomas Russell, the genial officer home on half pay; Samuel Nielson, draper and printer; Henry Joy McCracken, a Presbyterian cotton manufacturer; the ubiquitous ideologue Dr William Drennan . . . the Dublin leaders included Thomas Addis Emmet, son of a state physician, a lawyer; Dr Rowan Hamilton; Oliver Bond, a woollen merchant; John and Henry Sheares, lawyers; John Sweetman, brewer, and Arthur O'Connor, Trinity-educated son of a merchant family.

Connolly's description of the politics of later republican leaders contains the same ambiguity. Fintan Lalor is proclaimed 'an apostle of Irish revolutionary socialism', and is mentioned for his call to tenants to refuse rent to their landlords — but his defence of the rights of private property is not mentioned. John Mitchel is praised for his support for the February 1848 revolution in France. But when Mitchel, like his French republican counterparts, drew back in horror when workers took the initiative in the revolution, Connolly excuses this, saying Mitchel had received 'garbled reports'. Similarly Connolly rightly shows the coincidence of the growth of the Fenians with the first stirrings of the labour movement — but doesn't analyse the politics of Fenianism itself.

What we have here is Connolly's attempt to take back the republican tradition for the left. To do this, he had to gloss over the movement's radical capitalist origins. Instead he focussed on its popular base among the urban and rural poor. But by glossing over the origins of republicanism Connolly was led to an over-optimistic perspective about how far to the left the republican tradition could move. He failed to see that republicanism set limits upon itself. Unlike Lenin, who polemicised against a similar tradition in rural Russia, the *Narodniks*, Connolly's optimism led him to stress the common ground that socialists and republicans shared — since by doing this he believed it would make the shift to the left easier.

In Connolly's defence it must be said that no socialist operating within a colonised country had come near to tackling this issue. It is only with the benefit of hindsight, seeing the experience not only of the struggle in Ireland but also the independence struggles of countries such as Zimbabwe, Algeria and Angola, that we have come to understand the limitations of radical nationalism. From this experience we can see today the necessity for Irish socialists both to struggle alongside republicans against imperialism *and* to subject republican political ideas and activities to merciless criticism.

Connolly's achievement was that he laid the foundation stone for a revolutionary socialist strategy in Ireland. Writing in virtual isolation, his view of the role of the working class in the struggle for national liberation shared common ground with that of the Russian revolutionary Leon Trotsky. In his theory of permanent revolution, Trotsky argued that in backward countries only the working class would fight consistently to remove the shackles of feudalism and imperialism. But, he added, this struggle would end successfully only if it concluded with the establishment of a workers' state as the opening shot in an international socialist revolution.

Connolly grasped the first element of this. The great value of **Labour in Irish History** is that it spells out in detail Connolly's fundamental insight that 'the shifting of economic and political forces which accompanies the development of the system of capitalist society leads inevitably to the increasing conservation of the non-working class element, and to the revolutionary vigour and power of the working class', and that therefore '*only the working class remain as the incorruptible inheritors of the fight for freedom in Ireland*'.

This insight, which Connolly shared with Trotsky's analysis of Russian society, puts him head-and-shoulders over many later left-wing theorists who have sought in vain to find allies among 'progressive' sections of the Irish upper class.

Connolly's insight, however, was not translated into a clear strategy. Because he ruled out the possibility of further capitalist development in Ireland, he relied on a virtual 'iron law of history' to transform the raw elements of republicanism into full-blooded revolutionary socialism. The essential political argument — that the goal of struggle in Ireland should be not simply a republic, but a *workers'* republic — was missing. For these reasons, socialists seeking a strategy for Ireland today should follow a reading of **Labour in Irish History** with that of Trotsky's **Permanent Revolution**.

This is not to detract from Connolly's achievements. His arguments hold a continued relevance for Marxists and socialists today, both in Ireland and elsewhere. His writings are an embarrassment to those sections of the left who oppose the struggle against the Orange state of the north on the grounds that they oppose nationalism. His writings also offer a challenge to the left inside Sinn Fein, for Connolly's thorough-going class politics expose the limitations of a republican leadership which calls for alliances with the 'green Tories' of Fianna Fail. For this reason they should be read today by all who would fight for the freedom of Ireland.

Kieran Allen

LABOUR IN IRISH HISTORY

AUTHOR'S FOREWORD

IN HER great work, **The Making of Ireland and its Undoing**, the only contribution to Irish history we know of which conforms to the methods of modern historical science, the authoress, Mrs Stopford Green, dealing with the effect upon Ireland of the dispersion of the Irish race in the time of Henry VIII and Elizabeth, and the consequent destruction of Gaelic Culture, and rupture with Gaelic tradition and law, says that the Irishmen educated in schools abroad abandoned or knew nothing of the lore of ancient Erin, and had no sympathy with the spirit of the Brehon Code, nor with the social order of which it was the juridical expression. She says they 'urged the theory, so *antagonistic to the immemorial law of Ireland*, that only from the polluted sinks of heretics could come the idea that the people might elect a ruler, and confer supreme authority on whomsoever pleased them'. In other words the new Irish, educated in foreign standards, had adopted as their own the feudal-capitalist system of which England was the exponent in Ireland, and urged it upon the Gaelic Irish. As the dispersion of the class, consummated by Cromwell, finally completed the ruin of Gaelic Ireland, all the higher education of Irishmen thenceforward ran in this foreign groove, and was coloured with this foreign colouring.

In other words, the Gaelic culture of the Irish chieftainry was rudely broken off in the seventeenth century, and the Continental schools of European despots implanted in its place in the minds of the Irish students, and sent them back to Ireland to preach a fanatical belief in royal and feudal prerogatives, as foreign to the genius of the Gael as was the English ruler to Irish soil. What a light this sheds upon Irish history of the seventeenth, eighteenth and nineteenth centuries! And what a commentary it is upon the real origin of that so-called 'Irish veneration for the aristocracy', of which the bourgeois charlatans of Irish literature write so eloquently! That veneration is seen to be as much of an exotic, as much of an importation, as the aristocratic caste it venerated. Both were

. . . foul foreign blossoms
Blown hither to poison our plains.

But so deeply has this insidious lie about the aristocratic tendencies of the Irish taken root in Irish thought that it will take a long time to eradicate it from the minds of the people, or to make the Irish realise that the whole concept of orthodox Irish history for the last 200 years was a betrayal and abandonment of the best traditions of the Irish race. Yet such is undoubtedly the case. Let us examine this a little more closely.

Just as it is true that a stream cannot rise above its source, so it is true that a national literature cannot rise above the moral level of the social conditions of the people from whom it derives its inspiration. If we would understand the national literature of a people we must study their social and political status, keeping in mind the fact that their writers were a product thereof, and that the children of their brains were conceived and brought forth in certain historical conditions. Ireland at the same time as she lost her ancient social system, also lost her language as the vehicle of thought of those who acted as her leaders. As a result of this twofold loss the nation suffered socially, nationally and intellectually from a prolonged arrested development. During the closing years of the seventeenth century, all the eighteenth, and the greater part of the nineteenth, the Irish people were the lowest helots in Europe, socially and politically. The Irish peasant, reduced from the position of a free clansman owning his tribelands and controlling its administration in common with his fellows, was a mere tenant-at-will subject to eviction, dishonour and outrage at the hands of an irresponsible private proprietor. Politically he was non-existent, legally he held no rights, intellectually he sank under the weight of his social abasement, and surrendered to the downward drag of his poverty. He had been conquered, and he suffered all the terrible consequences of defeat at the hands of a ruling class and nation who have always acted upon the old Roman maxim of 'Woe to the vanquished'.

To add to his humiliation, those of his name and race who had contrived to escape the general ruin, and sent their children to be educated in foreign schools, discovered with the return of those 'wild geese' to their native habitat that they who had sailed for France, Italy or Spain, filled with hatred of the English Crown and of the English landlord garrison in Ireland, returned as mere Catholic adherents of a pretender to the English throne, using all the prestige of their foreign schooling to discredit the Gaelic ideas of equality and democracy, and instead instilling into the minds of the growing generation feudal ideas of the divine right of kings to rule, and of subjects to unquestioningly obey. The Irish students in the universities of the Continent were the first products of a scheme which the Papacy still pursues with its accustomed skill and persistence — a persistence which recks little of the passing centuries — a scheme which looks upon Catholic Ireland simply as a tool to be used for the spiritual re-conquest of England to Catholicity. In the eighteenth century this scheme did its deadliest work in Ireland. It failed ridiculously to cause a single Irish worker in town or country to strike a blow for the Stuart cause in the years of the Scottish Rebellions of 1715 and 1745 but it prevented them from striking any blows for their own cause, or from taking advantage of the civil feuds of their enemies. It did more. It killed Gaelic Ireland; an Irish-speaking Catholic was of no value as a missionary of Catholicism in England, and an Irish peasant who treasured the tongue of his fathers might also have some reverence for the principles of the social polity and and civilisation under which his forefathers had lived and prospered for unnumbered years. And such principles were even more distasteful to French, Spanish or Papal patrons of Irish schools of learning on the Continent than they were to English monarchs. Thus the poor Irish were not only pariahs in the social system of their day, but they were also precluded from hoping for a revival of intellectual life through the achievements of their children. Their children were taught to despise the language and traditions of their fathers.

It was at or during this period, when the Irish peasant had been crushed to the very lowest point when the most he could hope for was to be pitied as animals are pitied; it was during this period Irish literature in English was born. Such Irish literature was not written for Irishmen, as a real Irish literature would be, it was written by Irishmen, about Irishmen, but for English or Anglo-Irish consumption.

Hence the Irishman in English literature may be said to have been born with an apology in his mouth. His creators knew nothing of the free and independent Irishman of Gaelic Ireland, but they did know the conquered, robbed, slave-driven, brutalised, demoralised Irishman, the product of generations of landlord and capitalist rule, and him they seized upon, held up to the gaze of the world, and asked the nations to accept as the true Irish type.

If he crouched before a representative of royalty with an abject submission born of a hundred years of political outlawry and training in foreign ideas, his abasement was pointed to proudly as an instance of the 'ancient Celtic fidelity to hereditary monarchs'; if with the memory of perennial famines, evictions, jails, hangings, and tenancy-at-will beclouding his brain he humbled himself before the upper class, or attached himself like a dog to their personal fortunes, his sycophancy was cited as a manifestation of 'ancient Irish veneration for the aristocracy', and if long-continued insecurity of life begat in him a fierce desire for the ownership of a piece of land to safeguard his loved ones in a system where land was life, this new-born land-hunger was triumphantly trumpeted forth as a proof of the 'Irish attachment to the principle of private property'. Be it understood we are not talking now of the English slanderers of the Irishman, but of his Irish apologists. The English slanderer never did as much harm as did these self-constituted delineators of Irish characteristics. The English slanderer lowered Irishmen in the eyes of the world, but his Irish middle-class teachers and writers lowered him in his own eyes by extolling as an Irish virtue every sycophantic vice begotten of generations of slavery. Accordingly, as an Irishman, peasant, labourer, or artisan, banded himself with his fellows to strike back at their oppressors in defence of their right to live in the land of their fathers, the 'respectable' classes who had imbibed the foreign ideas publicly deplored his act, and unctuously ascribed it to the 'evil effects of English misgovernment upon the Irish character'; but when an occasional Irishman, abandoning all the traditions of his race, climbed up upon the backs of his fellows to wealth or position, his career was held up as a sample of what Irishmen could do under congenial or favourable circumstances. The seventeenth, eighteenth and nineteenth centuries were, indeed, the *Via Dolorosa* of the Irish race. In them the Irish Gael sank out of sight, and in his place the middle-class politicians, capitalists and ecclesiastics laboured to produce a hybrid Irishman, assimilating a foreign social system, a foreign speech, and a foreign character. In the effort to assimilate the first two the Irish were unhappily too successful, so successful that today the majority of the Irish do not know that their fathers ever knew another system of ownership, and the Irish Irelanders are painfully grappling with their mother tongue with the hesitating accent of a foreigner. Fortunately the Irish character has proven too difficult to press into respectable foreign moulds, and the recoil of that character from the deadly embrace of capitalist English conventionalism, as it has already led to a revaluation of the speech of the Gael, will in all probability also lead to a re-study and appreciation of the social system under which the Gael reached the highest point of civilisation and culture in Europe.

In the re-conversion of Ireland to the Gaelic principle of common ownership by a people of their sources of food and maintenance, the worst obstacle to overcome will be the opposition of the men and women who have imbibed their ideas of Irish character and history from Anglo-Irish literature. That literature, as we have explained, was born in the worst agonies of the slavery of our race; it bears all the birth-marks of such origin upon it, but irony of ironies, these birth-marks of slavery are hailed by our teachers as 'the native characteristics of the Celt'.

One of these slave birth-marks is a belief in the capitalist system of society; the Irishman frees himself from such a mark of slavery when he realises the truth that the capitalist system is the most foreign thing in Ireland.

Hence we have had in Ireland for over 250 years the remarkable phenomenon of Irishmen of the upper and middle classes urging upon the Irish toilers as a sacred national and religious duty the necessity of maintaining a social order against which their Gaelic forefathers had struggled, despite prison cells, famine, and the sword, for over 400 years. Reversing the procedure of the Normans settled in Ireland who were said to have become 'more Irish than the Irish', the Irish propertied classes became more English than the English, and so have continued to our day.

Hence we believe that this book, attempting to depict the attitude of the dispossessed masses of the Irish people in the great crisis of modern Irish history, may justly be looked upon as part of the literature of the Gaelic revival. As the Gaelic language, scorned by the possessing classes, sought and found its last fortress in the hearts and homes of the 'lower orders', to re-issue from thence in our own time what the writer believes to be a greater and more enduring place in civilisation than of old, so in the words of Thomas Francis Meagher, the same 'wretched cabins have been the holy shrines in which the traditions and the hopes of Ireland have been treasured and transmitted'.

The apostate patriotism of the Irish capitalist class, arising as it does upon the rupture with Gaelic tradition, will, of course, reject this conception, and saturated with foreignism themselves, they will continue to hurl the epithet of 'foreign ideas' against the militant Irish democracy. But the present and more analytical study of the laws and social structure of Ireland before the English invasion, amongst its other good results, will have this one also, that it will conform and establish the truth of this conception. Hitherto the study of the social structure of Ireland in the past has been marred by one great fault. For a description and interpretation of Irish social life and customs the student depended entirely upon the description and interpretation of men who were entirely lacking in knowledge of, and insight into, the facts and spirit of the things they attempted to describe. Imbued with the conception of feudalistic or capitalistic social order, the writers perpetually strove to explain Irish institutions in terms of an order of things to which those institutions were entirely alien. Irish titles, indicative of the function in society performed by their bearers, the writers explained by what they supposed were analogous titles in the feudal order of England, forgetful of the fact as the one form of society was the antithesis of the other, and not its counterpart, the one set of titles could not possibly convey the same meaning as the other, much less be a translation.

Much the same mistake was made in America by the early Spanish conquistadors in attempting to describe the social and political systems of Mexico and Peru, with much the same results of introducing almost endless confusion into every attempt to comprehend life as it actually existed in those countries before the conquest. The Spanish writers could not mentally raise themselves out of the social structure of Continental Europe, and hence their weird and wonderful tales of despotic Peruvian and Mexican 'Emperors' and 'Nobles' where really existed the elaborately organised family system of a people not yet fully evolved into the political state. Not until the publication of Morgan's monumental work on **Ancient Society** was the key to the study of American native civilisation really found and placed in the hands of the student. The same key will yet unlock the doors which guard the secrets of our native Celtic civilisation, and make them possible of fuller comprehension for the multitude.

Meanwhile, we desire to place before our readers the two propositions upon which this book is founded — propositions which we believe embody alike the fruits of the experience of the past and the matured thought of the present upon the points under consideration.

First, that in the evolution of civilisation the progress of the fight for national liberty of any subject nation must, perforce, keep pace with the progress of the struggle for liberty of the most subject class in that nation, and that the shifting of economic and political forces which accompanies the development of the system of capitalist society leads inevitably to the increasing conservation of the non-working class element, and to the revolutionary vigour and power of the working class.

Second, that the result of the long drawn out struggle of Ireland has been, so far, that the old chieftainry has disappeared, or through its degenerate descendants has made terms with iniquity, and become part and parcel of the supporters of the established order; the middle class, growing up in the midst of the national struggle, and at one time, as in 1798, through the stress of the economic rivalry of England almost forced into the position of revolutionary leaders against the despotism of their industrial competitors, have now also bowed the knee to Baal, and have a thousand economic strings in the shape of investments binding them to English capitalism as against every sentimental or historic attachment drawing them towards Irish patriotism; only the Irish working class remain as the incorruptible inheritors of the fight for freedom in Ireland.

To that unconquered Irish working class this book is dedicated by one of their number.

JAMES CONNOLLY

Chapter One

THE LESSONS OF HISTORY

'What is History but a fable agreed upon.' — *Napoleon I*

IT IS in itself a significant commentary upon the subordinate place allotted to labour in Irish politics that a writer should think it necessary to explain his purpose before setting out to detail for the benefit of his readers the position of the Irish workers in the past, and the lessons to be derived from a study of that position in guiding the movement of the working class today.

Were history what it ought to be, an accurate literary reflex of the times with which it professes to deal, the pages of history would be almost entirely engrossed with a recital of the wrongs and struggles of the labouring people, constituting, as they have ever done, the vast mass of mankind. But history, in general, treats the working class as the manipulator of politics treats the working man — that is to say with contempt when he remains passive, and with derision, hatred and misrepresentation whenever he dares to evince a desire to throw off the yoke of political or social servitude. Ireland is no exception to the rule. Irish history has ever been written by the master class — in the interests of the master class.

Whenever the social question cropped up in modern Irish history, whenever the question of labour and its wrongs figured in the writings or speeches of our modern Irish politicians, it was simply that they might be used as weapons in the warfare against a political adversary, and not at all the person so using them was personally convinced that the subjection of labour was in itself a wrong.

The present series of articles* are intended primarily to prove that contention. To prove it by a reference to the evidence — documentary and otherwise — adduced illustrating the state of the Irish working class in the past, the almost total indifference of our Irish politicians to the sufferings of the mass of the people, and the true inwardness of many of the political agitations which have occupied the field in the eighteenth and nineteenth centuries. Special attention is given to the period preceding the Union,** and evidence brought forward relative to the state of Ireland before and during the continuance of Grattan's Parliament; to the condition of the working people in town and country, and the attitude towards labour taken up by politicians of all sides, whether patriot or ministerialist.

In other words, we propose to do what in us lies to repair the deliberate neglect of the social question by our historians, and to prepare the way in order that other and abler pens than our own may demonstrate to the reading public the manner in which economic conditions have controlled and dominated our Irish history.

But as a preliminary to this essay on our part it becomes necessary to recapitulate here some of the salient facts of history we have elsewhere insisted upon as essential to a thorough grasp of the 'Irish Question'.

Politically, Ireland has been under the control of England for the past 700 years, during the greater part of which time the country has been the scene of constant wars against her rule upon the part of the native Irish. Until the year 1649, these wars were complicated by the fact that they were directed against both the political and *social* order recognised by the English invader. It may surprise many readers to learn that up to the date above-mentioned the basis of society in Ireland, except within the Pale (a small strip of territory around the capital city, Dublin), rested upon communal or tribal ownership of land. The Irish chief, although recognised in the courts of France, Spain and Rome, as the peer of the reigning princes of Europe, in reality held his position upon the sufferance of

*__Labour in Irish History__ first appeared as a series of articles in **The Harp**, a journal first published by Connolly in the US, and in **Workers' Republic**.
**The Act of Union between Britain and Ireland, passed by parliament in 1800.

his people, and as an administrator of the tribal affairs of his people, while the land or territory of the clan was entirely removed from his private jurisdiction.

In the parts of Ireland where for 400 years after the first conquest (so-called) the English governors could not penetrate except at the head of a powerful army, the social order which prevailed in England was unknown, and as this comprised the greater portion of the country, it gradually came to be understood that the war against the foreign oppressor was also a war against private property in land. But with the forcible break up of the clan system in 1649, the social aspect of the Irish struggle sank out of sight, its place being usurped by the mere political expressions of the fight for freedom.

Such an event was of course inevitable in any case. Communal ownership of land would, undoubtedly, have given way to the privately owned system of capitalist-landlordism, even if Ireland had remained an independent country, but coming as it did in obedience to the pressure of armed force from without, instead of by the operation of economic forces from within, the change has been bitterly and justly resented by the vast mass of the Irish people, many of whom still mix with their dreams of liberty longings for a return to the ancient system of land tenure — now organically impossible.

The dispersion of the clans, of course, put an end to the leadership of the chiefs, and in consequence, the Irish aristocracy *being all of foreign or traitor origin*, Irish patriotic movements fell entirely into the hands of the middle class, and became, for the most part, simply idealised expressions of middle-class interest.

Hence the spokesmen of the middle class, in the press and on the platform, have consistently sought the emasculation of the Irish national movement, the distortion of Irish history, and, above all, the denial of all relation between the social rights of the Irish nation. It was hoped and intended by this means to create what is termed 'a real national movement' — i.e. a movement in which each class would recognise the rights of the other classes and laying aside their contentions would unite in a national struggle against the common enemy — England.

Needless to say, the only class deceived by such phrases was the working class. When questions of 'class' interests are eliminated from public controversy a victory is thereby gained for the possessing, conservative class, whose only hope of security lies in such elimination. Like a fraudulent trustee, the bourgeois dreads nothing so much as an impartial and rigid inquiry into the validity of his title deeds. Hence the bourgeois press and politicians incessantly strive to inflame the working-class mind to fever heat upon questions outside the range of their own class interests. War, religion, race, language, political reform, patriotism — apart from whatever intrinsic merits they may possess — all serve in the hands of the possessing class as counter-irritants, whose functions by engendering heat in such parts of the body politic as are farthest removed from the seat of economic enquiry, and consequently of class consciousness on the part of the proletariat. The bourgeois Irishman has long been an adept at such manoeuvring, and has, it must be confessed, found in his working-class countrymen exceedingly pliable material.

During the last hundred years every generation in Ireland has witnessed an attempted rebellion against English rule. Every such conspiracy or rebellion has drawn the majority of its adherence from the lower orders in town and country, yet under the inspiration of a few middle-class doctrinaires the social question has been religiously excluded from the field of action to be covered by the rebellion if successful; in hopes that by such exclusion it would be possible to conciliate the upper classes and enlist them in the struggle for freedom.

The result has in nearly every case been the same. The workers, though furnishing the greatest proportion of recruits to the ranks of the revolutionists, and consequently of victims to the prison and the scaffold, could not be imbued *en masse* with the revolutionary fire necessary to seriously imperil a dominion rooted for 700 years in the heart of their country. They were all anxious enough for freedom but realising the enormous odds against them, and being explicitly told by their leaders that they *must not expect any change in their condition of social subjection, even if successful*, they as a body shrank from the contest, and left only the purest minded and most chivalrous of their class to face the odds and glut the vengeance of the tyrant — a warning to those in all countries who neglect the vital truth that successful revolutions are not the product of our brains, but of ripe material conditions.

The upper class also turned a contemptuously deaf ear to the charming of the bourgeois patriot. They (the upper class) naturally clung to their property, landed and otherwise; under the protecting power of England they felt themselves secure in the possession thereof, but were by no means assured as to the fate which might befall it in a successful revolutionary uprising. The landlord class, therefore, remained absolutely loyal to England, and while the middle-class poets and romanticists were enthusing on the hope of a 'union of class and creeds', the aristocracy were pursuing their private interests against their tenants with a relentlessness which threatened to depopulate the country, and led even an English Conservative newspaper, the London **Times**, to declare that 'the name of an Irish landlord stinks in the nostrils of Christendom.'

It is well to remember, as a general warning against similar foolishness in future, the the generation of Irish landlords which had listened to the eloquent pleadings of Thomas Davis* was the same as that which in the Famine years 'exercised its rights with a rod of iron and renounced its duties with a front of brass.'

The lower middle class gave to the national cause in the past many unselfish patriots, but, on the whole, while willing and ready enough to please their humble fellow-countrymen, and to compound with their own conscience by shouting louder than all others their untiring devotion to the cause of freedom, they, as a class, unceasingly strove to divert the public mind upon the lines of constitutional agitation for such reforms as might remove irritating and unnecessary officialism, while leaving untouched the basis of national and economic subjection.

This policy enables them to masquerade as patriots before the unthinking multitude, and at the same time lends greater force to their words when as 'patriot leaders' they cry down any serious revolutionary movement that might demand from them greater proof of sincerity than can be furnished by the strength of their

*Thomas Davis was leader of the Young Ireland movement in the 1840s. He was also a poet.

lungs, or greater sacrifices than would be suitable to their exchequer. 1848 and 1867, the Young Ireland and the Fenian Movements, furnish the classic illustration of this policy on the part of the Irish middle class.

Such, then, is our view of Irish politics and Irish history. Subsequent chapters will place before our readers the facts upon which such a view is based.

Chapter Two

THE JACOBITES AND THE IRISH PEOPLE

'If ever there was a time when it behoved men in public stations to be explicit, if ever there was a time when *those scourges of the human race called politicians* should lay aside their duplicity and finesse, it is the present moment. Be assured that the people of this country will no longer bear that their welfare should be the sport of a few family factions; be assured they are convinced their true interest consists of putting down men of self creation, who have no object in view but that of aggrandising themselves and their families at the expense of the public, and in setting up men who shall represent the nation, who shall be accountable to the nation, and who shall do the business of the nation.' — *Arthur O'Connor in the Irish House of Commons*, 4 May 1795.

MODERN IRISH history properly understood may be said to start with the close of the Williamite Wars in the year 1691. All the political life of Ireland during the next 200 years draws its colouring from, and can only be understood in the light of that conflict between King James of England and the claimant for his throne, William, Prince of Orange. Our Irish politics even to this day and generation have been and are largely determined by the light in which the different sections of the Irish people regarded the prolonged conflict which closed with the surrender of Sarsfield* and the garrison to the investing forces of the Williamite party.

*Patrick Sarsfield was the leading officer of the Irish Jacobite forces.

Yet never in all the history of Ireland has there been a war in which the people of Ireland had less reason to be interested either on one side or the other. It is unfortunately beyond all question that the Irish Catholics shed their blood like water and wasted their wealth like dirt in an effort to retain King James upon the throne. But it is equally beyond all question that the whole struggle was no earthly concern of theirs; that King James was one of the most worthless representatives of a race that ever sat upon the throne; that the 'pious, glorious and immortal' William was a mere adventurer fighting for his own hand, and his army recruited from the impecunious swordsmen of Europe who cared as little for Protestantism as they did for human life; and that neither army had the slightest claim to be considered as a patriot army combating for the freedom of the Irish race.

So far from the paeans of praise lavished upon Sarsfield and the Jacobite army being justified, it is questionable whether a more enlightened or patriotic age than our own will not condemn them as little better than traitors for their action in seducing the Irish people from their allegiance to the cause of their country's freedom to plunge them into a war on behalf of a foreign tyrant — a tyrant who, even in the midst of their struggles on his behalf, opposed the Dublin parliament in its efforts to annul the supremacy of the English parliament.

The war between William and James offered a splendid opportunity to the subject people of Ireland to make a bid for freedom while the forces of their oppressors were rent in civil war. The opportunity was cast aside, and the subject people took sides on behalf of the opposing factions of their enemies.

The reason is not hard to find. The Catholic gentlemen and nobles who had the leadership of the people of Ireland at the time were, one and all, men who possessed considerable property in the country, property to which they had, notwithstanding their Catholicity, *no more right to title than the merest Cromwellian or Williamite adventurer*. The lands they held were lands which in former times belonged to the Irish people — in other words, they were tribe-lands. As such, the peasantry — then reduced to the position of mere tenants at will — were the rightful owners of the soil, while the Jacobite chivalry of

King James were either the descendants of men who had taken sides with the oppressor against their own countrymen and were allowed to retain their property as the fruits of treason; or finally, of men who had consented to seek from the English government for a grant giving them a personal title to the lands of their clansmen.

From such a combination no really national action could be expected, and from first to last of their public proceedings they acted as an English faction and as an English faction only. In whatever point they might disagree with the Williamites, they were at least in perfect accord with them on one point — viz., that the Irish people should be a subject people; and it will be readily understood that even had the war ended in the complete defeat of William and the triumph of James, the lot of the Irish, whether as tillers of the soil or as a nation, would not have been substantially improved.

The undeniable patriotism of the rank and file does not alter the truthfulness of the situation. They saw only the new enemy from England; the old English enemy settled in Ireland they were generously, but foolishly, ready to credit with all the virtues and attributes of patriotic Irishmen.

To further illustrate our point regarding the character of the Jacobite leaders in Ireland we might adduce the result of the great land settlement of Ireland in 1675. Eleven million acres had been surveyed at that time, of which four million acres were in the possession of Protestant settlers as the result of previous confiscations.

Lands so held were never disturbed, but the remainder were distributed as follows:

	Acres
To soldiers who had served in the Irish Wars	2,367,715
To 49 officers	497,001
To adventurers (who had lent money)	707,321
To provisors (to whom land had been promised)	477,873
To Duke of Ormond and Colonel Butler	257,518
To Duke of York	169,436
To Protestant Bishops	31,526

The lands left to the Catholics were distributed among the Catholic 'gentlemen' as follows:

	Acres
To those who were declared 'innocent' — that is to say, those who had not fought for freedom, but had sided with the government	1,176,570
To provisors (land promised)	497,001
Nominees in possession	68,260
Restitutions	55,396
To those transferred to Connaught, under James I	541,330

It will thus be seen that, with the exception of the lands held in Connaught, all the lands held by the Catholic gentry throughout Ireland were lands gained in the manner we have before described — as the spoils of conquest or the fruits of treachery. Even in that province the lands of the gentry were held under a feudal tenure from the English Crown, and therefore their owners had entered into a direct agreement with the invader to set aside the rights of the clan community in favour of their own personal claims.

Here then was the real reason for the refusal of the Irish leaders of that time to raise the standard of the Irish nation instead of the banner of an English faction. They fought not for freedom for Ireland, not for the restitution of their rights to the Irish people, but rather to secure that the class who then enjoyed the privilege of robbing the Irish people should not be compelled to give way in their turn to a fresh horde of land thieves.

Much has been made of their attempt to repeal Poyning's Law* and in other ways to give greater legislative force to the resolutions of the Dublin parliament, as if such acts were a proof of their sincere desire to free the country, and not merely to make certain their own tenure of power. But such claims on the part of some writers are only another proof of the difficulty of comprehending historical occurrences without having some central principle to give and direct in the task.

For the benefit of our readers we may here set forth the socialist key to the pages of history in order that it may be the more readily understood why in the past the governing classes have ever and always

*Poyning's Law made the Dublin parliament subordinate to the parliament in London.

aimed at the conquest of political power as the guarantee for their economic domination — or, to put it more plainly, for the social subjection of the masses — and why the freedom of the workers, even in a political sense, must be incomplete and insecure until they wrest from the governing classes the possession of the land and instruments of wealth production. This proposition, or key to history, as set forth by Karl Marx, the greatest of modern thinkers and first of scientific socialists, is as follows:

> That in every historical epoch the prevailing method of economic production and exchange, and the social organisation necessarily following from it, forms the basis upon which alone can be explained the political and intellectual history of that epoch.

In Ireland at the time of the Williamite war the 'prevailing method of economic production and exchange' was the feudal method based upon the private ownership of lands stolen from the Irish people, and all the political struggles of the period were built upon the material interests of one set of usurpers who wished to retain, and another set who wished to obtain, the mastery of those lands — in other words, the application of such a key as the above to the problem furnished by the Jacobite parliament of King James at once explains the reason of the so-called patriotic efforts of the Catholic gentry. Their efforts were directed to the conservation of their own rights of property, as against the right of the English parliament to interfere with or regulate such rights.

The so-called Patriotic Parliament was in reality, like every other that ever sat in Dublin, merely a collection of land thieves and their lackeys; their patriotism consisted in an effort to retain for themselves the spoils of the native peasantry; the English influence against which they protested was the influence of their fellow thieves in England hungry for a share of the spoil; and Sarsfield and his followers did not become Irish patriots because of their fight against King William's government any more than an Irish Whig out of office become a patriot because of his hatred to the Tories who are in.

The forces which battled beneath the walls of Derry or Limerick were not the forces of England and Ireland, but were the forces of two English political parties fighting for the possession of the powers of government; and the leaders of the Irish Wild Geese* on the battlefields of Europe were not shedding their blood because of their fidelity to Ireland, as our historians pretend to believe, but because they had attached themselves to the defeated side in English politics.

This fact was fully illustrated by the action of the old Franco-Irish at the time of the French Revolution. They in a body volunteered into the English army to help put down the new French Republic, and as a result Europe witnessed the spectacle of the new republican Irish exiles fighting for the French Revolution, and the sons of the old aristocratic Irish exiles fighting under the banner of England to put down that revolution. It is time we learned to appreciate and value the truth upon such matters, and to brush from our eyes the cobwebs woven across them by our ignorant or unscrupulous history-writing politicians.

On the other hand, it is just as necessary to remember that King William, when he had finally subdued his enemies in Ireland, showed by his actions that he and his followers were animated throughout by the same class feeling and considerations as their opponents. When the war was over William confiscated a million and a half acres, and distributed them among the aristocratic plunderers who followed him as follows:

He gave Lord Bentinck 135,300 acres; Lord Albemarle, 103,603; Lord Conningsby, 59,667; Lord Romney, 49,517; Lord Galway, 36,142; Lord Athlone, 26,840; Lord Rochford, 49,512; Dr Leslie, 16,000; Mr. F. Keighley, 12,000; Lord Mountjoy, 12,000; Sir T. Prendergast, 7,083; Colonel Hamilton, 5,886 acres.

These are a few of the men whose descendants some presumably sane Irishmen imagine will be converted into 'nationalists' by preaching 'a union of classes'.

It must not be forgotten, also, if only as a proof of his religious sincerity, that King William bestowed 95,000 acres, plundered from the Irish people, upon his paramour, Elizabeth Villiers, Countess of

*The defeated soldiers were allowed to leave for France, where they formed an Irish Brigade to fight in the French army — where they became known as the Wild Geese.

Orkney. But the virtuous Irish parliament interfered, took back the land, and distributed it amongst their immediate friends, the Irish Loyalist adventurers.

Chapter Three

PEASANT REBELLIONS

'To permit a small class, whether alien or native, to obtain a monopoly of the land is an intolerable injustice; its continued enforcement is neither more nor less than a robbery of the hard and laborious earnings of the poor.' — *Irish People* (organ of the Fenian Brotherhood), 30 July 1864.

IN THE PRECEDING chapter we pointed out that the Williamite war in Ireland, from Derry to Limerick, was primarily a war for mastery over the Irish people, and that all questions of national or industrial freedom were ignored by the leaders on both sides as being presumably what their modern prototype would style 'beyond the pale of practical politics'.

When the nation had once more settled down to the pursuits of peace, and all fear of a Catholic or Jacobite rising had departed from the minds of even the most timorous squireen, the unfortunate tenantry of Ireland, whether Catholic or Protestant, were enlightened upon how little difference the war had made to their position as a subject class. The Catholic who had been so foolish as to adhere to the army of James could not, in the nature of things, expect much consideration from his conquerors and he received none — but he had the consolation of seeing that the rank and file of his Protestant enemies were treated little, if at all, better than himself.

When the hungry horde of adventurers who had brought companies to the service of William had glutted themselves with the plunder for which they had crossed the [Irish] Channel, they showed no more disposition to remember the claims of the common soldier — by the aid of whose sword they had climbed to power — than do our present rulers when they consign to the workhouse the shattered frames of the poor fools who, with murder and pillage, have won for their masters empire in India or Africa.

Before long the Protestant and Catholic tenants were suffering one common oppression. The question of political supremacy having been finally decided, the yoke of economic slavery was now laid unsparingly upon the backs of the labouring people. All religious sects suffered equally from this cause. The Penal Laws then in operation against the Catholics did indeed make the life of propertied Catholics more insecure than would otherwise have been the case; but to the vast mass of the population the misery and hardship entailed by the working out of economic laws were fraught with infinitely more suffering than it was at any time within the power of the Penal Laws to inflict.

As a matter of fact, the effect of the latter code in impoverishing wealthy Catholics has been much overrated. The class interests which at all times unite the propertied section of the community operated, to a large extent, to render impossible the application of the power of persecution to its full legal limits. Rich Catholics were quietly tolerated and generally received from the rich Protestants an amount of respect and forbearance which the latter would not at any time extend to their Protestant tenantry or work-people.

So far was this true that, like the Jew, some Catholics became notorious as moneylenders, and in the year 1763 a bill was introduced into the Irish House of Commons to give greater facilities to Protestants wishing to borrow money from Catholics. The bill proposed to enable Catholics to become mortgagees of landed estates in order that Protestants wishing to borrow money could give a mortgage upon their lands as security to the Catholic lender. The bill was defeated, but its introduction serves to show how little the Penal Laws had operated to prevent the accumulation of wealth by the Catholic propertied classes.

But the social system thus firmly rooted in the soil of Ireland — and accepted as righteous by the ruling class irrespective of religion — was a greater enemy to the prosperity and happiness of the people than any legislation religious bigotry could devise. Modern Irish politicians, inspired either by a blissful unconsciousness of the facts of history, or else sublimely indifferent to its teachings, are in the habit of tracing the misery of Ireland to the Legislative Union as its source, but the slightest possible acquaintance with ante-Union literature will reveal a record of famine, oppression, and injustice, due to economic causes, unsurpassed at any other stage of modern Irish history.

Thus Dean Swift, writing in 1729, in that masterpiece of sarcasm entitled 'A Modern Proposal for Preventing the Children of the Poor People of Ireland from becoming a Burden on their Parents or Country, and for making them Beneficial to the Public', was so moved by the spectacle of poverty and wretchedness that, although having no love for the people, for whom, indeed, he had no better name than 'the savage old Irish', he produced the most vehement and bitter indictment of the society of his day — and the most striking picture of hopeless despair — literature has yet revealed. Here is in effect his 'Proposal':

> It is a melancholy object to those who walk through this great town, or travel in the country, when they see the streets, the roads, and cabin doors crowded with beggars of the female sex, followed by three, four or six children, all in rags, and importuning every passenger for an alms . . . I do, therfore, offer it to public consideration that of the hundred and twenty thousand children already computed, twenty thousand may be reserved for a breed . . . that the remaining hundred thousand may at a year old be offered in sale to the persons of quality and fortune through the kingdom, always the mother to let them suck plentifully in the last month so as to render them plump and fat for a good table. A child will make two dishes at an entertainment for friends, and when the family dines alone the fore or hind quarters will make a reasonable dish; and seasoned with a little pepper or salt, will be very good boiled on the fourth day, especially in winter . . . I have already computed the charge of nursing a beggar's child (in which list I reckon *all cottage labourers, and four-fifths of the farmers*), to be about two shillings per annum, rags included; and I believe no gentleman would

refuse to give ten shillings for the carcase of a good fat child, which, as I have said, will make four dishes of excellent nutritious meat.

Sarcasm, truly, but how terrible must have been the misery which made even such sarcasm permissible! Great as it undoubtedly was, it was surpassed twelve years later in the famine of 1740, when no less a number than 400,000 are estimated to have perished of hunger or of the diseases which follow in the wake of hunger. This may seem an exaggeration, but the statement is amply borne out by contemporary evidence. Thus, Bishop Berkeley, of the Anglican Church, writing to a Mr Thomas Prior, of Dublin, in 1741, mentions that 'the other day I heard one from the county of Limerick say that whole villages were entirely dispeopled. About two months since I heard Sir Richard Cox say that five hundred were dead in the parish, though in a country, I believe, not very populous.' And a pamphlet entitled 'The Groans of Ireland', published in 1741, asserts, 'the universal scarcity was followed by fluxes and malignant fevers, which swept off multitudes of all sorts, so that whole villages were laid waste.'

This famine, be it remarked, like all modern famine, was solely attributable to economic causes; the poor of all religions and politics were equally sufferers; the rich of all religions and politics were equally exempt. It is also noteworthy, as illustrating the manner in which the hireling scribes of the propertied classes have written history, that while a voluminous literature has arisen round the Penal Laws — a subject of merely posthumous interest — a matter of such overwhelming importance, both historically and practically, as the predisposing cause of Irish famine can, as yet, claim no notice except scanty and unavoidable references in national history.

The country had not recovered from the direful effects of this famine when a further economic development once more plunged the inhabitants into the blackest despair. Disease having attacked and destroyed great quantities of cattle in England, the aristocratic rulers of that country — fearful lest the ensuing high price of meat should lead to a demand for higher wages on the part of the working classes in England — removed the embargo off Irish cattle, meat, butter and cheese at the English ports, thus partly establishing free trade in those articles between the two countries. The immediate result was that all such provisions brought such a price in England that tillage farming in Ireland became unprofitable by comparison, and every effort was accordingly made to transform arable land into sheep-walks or grazing lands.

The landlord class commenced evicting their tenants; breaking up small farms, and even seizing upon village common lands and pasture grounds all over the country with the most disastrous results to the labouring people and cottiers generally. Where a hundred families had reaped a sustenance from their small farms, or by hiring out their labour to the owners of large farms, a dozen shepherds now occupied their places.

Immediately there sprang up throughout Ireland numbers of secret societies in which the dispossessed people strove by lawless acts and violent methods to restrain the greed of their masters, and to enforce their own right to life. They met in large bodies, generally at midnight, and proceeded to tear down enclosures; to hough cattle;* to dig up and so render useless the pasture lands; to burn the houses of shepherds; and in short, to terrorise their social rulers into abandoning the policy of grazing in favour of tillage, and to give more employment to the labourers and more security to the cottier.

These secret organisations assumed different names and frequently adopted different methods, and it is now impossible to tell whether they possessed any coherent organisation or not. Throughout the South they were called Whiteboys, from the practice of wearing white shirts over their clothes when on their nocturnal expeditions. About the year 1762 they posted their notices on conspicuous places in the country districts — notably, Cork, Waterford, Limerick, and Tipperary — threatening vengeance against such persons as had incurred their displeasure as graziers, evicting landlords, etc. These proclamations were signed by an imaginary female, sometimes called '*Sive Oultagh*', sometimes 'Queen Sive and Her Subjects'.

Government warred upon these poor wretches in the most vindictive manner; hanging, shooting, transporting without mercy;

*To 'hough' means to disable, by cutting the animals' hamstrings.

raiding villages at dead of night for suspected Whiteboys, and dragging the poor creatures before magistrates who never condescended to hear any evidence in favour of the prisoners, but condemned them to whatever punishments their vindictive class spirit or impaired digestion might prompt.

The spirit of the ruling class against those poor slaves in revolt may be judged by two incidents exemplifying how Catholic and Protestant proprietors united to fortify injustice and preserve their privileges, even at a time when we have been led to believe that the Penal Laws formed an insuperable barrier against such union. In the year 1762 the government offered the sum of £100 for the capture of the first five Whiteboy chiefs. The Protestant inhabitants of the city of Cork offered in addition £300 for the chief, and £50 for each of his first five accomplices arrested. Immediately the wealthy Catholics of the same city added to the above sums a promise of £200 for the chief and £40 for each of his first five subordinates.

This was at a time when an English governor, Lord Chesterfield, declared that if the military had killed as many landlords as they did Whiteboys, they would have contributed more effectively to restore quiet, a remark which conveys some slight idea of the carnage made among the peasantry. Yet, Flood, the great Protestant 'patriot', he of whom Davis sings —

Bless Harry Flood, who nobly stood
By us through gloomy years.

in the Irish House of Commons in 1763 fiercely denounced the government for not killing enough of the Whiteboys. He called it 'clemency'.

Chapter Four

SOCIAL REVOLTS AND POLITICAL KITES AND CROWS

'When the aristocracy come forward the people fall backward; when the people come forward the aristocracy, fearful of being left behind, insinuate themselves into our ranks and rise into timid leaders or treacherous auxiliaries.' — *Secret Manifesto of Projectors of United Irish Society*, 1791.

IN THE NORTH of Ireland the secret organisations of the peasantry were known variously as Oakboys and Hearts of Steel or Steelboys. The former directed their efforts mainly against the system of compulsory road repairing by which they were required to contribute their unpaid labour for the upkeep of country roads; a system, needless to say, offering every opportunity to the country gentry to secure labour gratuitously for the embellishment of their estates and private roads on the pretext of serving public ends.

The Oakboy organisation was particularly strong in the counties of Monaghan, Armagh and Tyrone. In a pamphlet published about the year 1762, an account is given of a 'rising' of the peasantry in the first-named county and of the heroic exploits of the officer in command of the troops engaged in suppressing said rising, in a manner which irresistibly recalls the present-day accounts in the English newspapers of the punitive expeditions of the British army against the 'marauding' hill tribes of India or Dacoits of Burma. The work is entitled the 'True and Faithful Account of the Late Insurrections in the North, with a narrative of Colonel Coote's Campaign against the Oakboys in the County Monaghan', etc.

The historian tells how, on hearing of the 'rising', the brave

British officer set off with his men to the town of Castleblayney; how on his way thither he passed numerous bodies of the peasantry proceeding in the same direction, each with an oak bough or twig stuck in his hat as a sign of his treasonable sympathies; how on entering Castleblayney he warned the people to disperse, and only received defiant replies, and even hostile manifestations; how he then took refuge in the Market House and prepared to defend it if need be; and how, after occupying that stronghold all night, he found next morning the rebels had withdrawn from the town.

Next, there is an account of the same valiant General's entry into the town of Ballybay. Here he found all the houses shut against him, each house proudly displaying an oak bough in its windows, and all the people seemingly prepared to resist to the uttermost. Apparently determined to make an example, and so to strike terror, the valiant soldier and his men prepared to arrest the ringleader, and after a severe struggle, did succeed in breaking into some cabins of the poor people, and arresting some person, who was accordingly hauled off to the town of Monaghan, there to be dealt with according to the forms of a law from which every consideration of justice was rigorously excluded.

In the town of Clones, we are informed, the people openly withstood the royal forces in the market place, but were, of course, defeated. The Monaghan Oakboys were then driven across the borders of their own county into Armagh, where they made a last stand, but were attacked and defeated in a 'pitched battle', the severity of which may be gauged from the fact that no casualties were reported on the side of the troops.

But the general feelings of the people were so pronouncedly against the system of compulsory and unpaid labour on the roads that the government subsequently abolished the practice, and instituted a road rate providing for payment for such necessary labour by a tax upon owners and occupiers of property in the district. Needless to say, the poor peasants who were suffering martyrdom in prison for their efforts to remedy what the government had by such remedial legislation admitted to be an injustice, were left to rot in their cells — the usual fate of pioneers of reform.

The Steelboys were a more formidable organisation, and had

their strongholds in the counties of Down and Antrim. They were for the most part Presbyterian or other dissenters from the Established Church, and, like the Whiteboys, aimed at the abolition or reduction of tithes and the restriction of the system of consolidating farms for grazing purposes. They frequently appeared in arms, and moved with a certain degree of discipline, coming together from widely separated parts in obedience, apparently, to the orders of a common centre.

In the year 1772 six of their number were arrested and lodged in the town jail of Belfast. Their associates immediately mustered in thousands, and in open day marched upon that city, made themselves masters thereof, stormed the jail, and released their comrades. This daring action excited consternation in the ranks of the governing classes, troops were despatched on the spot, and every precaution taken to ensure the arrest of the leaders. Out of the numerous prisoners made a batch were selected for trial, but whether as a result of intimidation or because of their sympathy with the prisoners it is difficult to tell, the jury in Belfast refused to convict, and when the venue of the trial was changed to Dublin, the government was equally unfortunate.

The refusal of the juries to convict was, probably, in a large measure due to the unpopularity of the Act then just introduced to enable the government to put persons accused of agrarian offences on trial in a different county to their own. When this Act was repealed the convictions and executions went on as merrily as before. Many a peasant's corpse swung on the gibbet, and many a promising life was doomed to blight and decay in the foul confines of the prison cell, to glut the vengeance of the dominant clases. Arthur Young, in his **Tour of Ireland**, thus describes the state of matters against which those poor peasants revolted.

> A landlord in Ireland can scarcely invent an order which a servant, labourer, or cottier dares to refuse to execute . . . Disrespect, or anything tending towards sauciness he may punish with his cane or his horsewhip with the most perfect security. A poor man would have his bones broken if he offered to lift a hand in his own defence . . . Landlords of consequence

have assured me that many of their cottiers would think themselves honoured by having their wives and daughters sent for to the bed of their master — a mark of slavery which proves the oppression under which such people must live.

It will be observed by the attentive student that the 'patriots' who occupied the public stage in Ireland during the period we have been dealing with never once raised their voices in protest against such social injustice. Like their imitators today they regarded the misery of the Irish people as a convenient handle for political agitation; and, like their imitators today, they were ever ready to outvie even the government in their denunciation of all those who, more earnest than themselves, sought to find a radical cure for such misery.

Of the trio of patriots — Swift, Molyneux and Lucas* — it may be noted that their fight was simply a repetition of the fight waged by Sarsfield and his followers in their day — a change of persons and of stage costume truly, but no change of character; a battle between the kites and the crows.

They found themselves members of a privileged class, living upon the plunder of the Irish people, but early perceived, to their dismay, that they could not maintain their position as a privileged class without the aid of the English army; and in return for supplying that army the English ruling class were determined to have the lion's share of the plunder.

The Irish parliament was essentially an English institution; nothing like it existed before the Norman Conqest. In that respect it was on the same footing as landlordism, capitalism, and their natural-born child — pauperism. England sent a swarm of adventurers to conquer Ireland; having partly succeeded these adventurers established a parliament to settle disputes among themselves, to contrive measures for robbing the natives, and to prevent their fellow-tyrants who had stayed in England from claiming the spoil.

But in course of time the section of land thieves resident in England did claim a right to supervise the doings of the adventurers

*Swift (Jonathan Swift the poet), Molyneux and Lucas were leaders of the Protestant establishment in Ireland.

in Ireland, and consequently to control their parliament. Hence arose Poyning's Law, and the subordination of Dublin parliament to the London parliament. Finding this subordinate position of their parliament enabled the English ruling class to strip the Irish workers of the fruits of their toil, the more far-seeing of the privileged class in Ireland became alarmed lest the stripping process should go too far, and leave nothing for them to fatten upon.

At once they becme patriots, anxious that Ireland — which, in their phraseology, meant the ruling class in Ireland — should be free from the control of the parliament of England. Their pamphlets, speeches, and all public pronouncements were devoted to telling the world how much nicer, equitable, and altogether more delectable it would be for the Irish people to be robbed in the interests of native-born aristocracy being compelled to divide the plunder with its English rival.

Perhaps Swift, Molyneux, or Lucas did not confess even to themselves that such was the basis of their political creed. The human race has at all times shown a proneness to gloss over its basest actions with a multitude of specious pretences, and to cover even its inequities with the glamour of a false sentimentality. But we are not dealing with appearances but realities, and, in justice to ourselves, we must expose the flimsy sophistry which strives to impart to a sordid, self-seeking struggle the appearance of a patriotic movement. In opposition to the movement of the people the patriot politicians and government alike were an undivided mass.

In their fight against tithes the Munster peasantry, in 1786, issued a remarkable document, which we here reprint as an illustration of the thought of the people of the provinces of that time. This document was copied into many papers at the time and was also reprinted in a pamphlet in October of that year.

Letter addressed to Munster peasantry

'To obviate the bad impression made by the calumnies of our enemies, we beg leave to submit to you our claim for the protection of humane gentry and humbly solicit yours, if said claim shall appear to you founded in justice and good policy.

'In every age, country and religion the priesthood are allowed to have been artful, usurping, and tenacious of their ill-acquired prerogatives. Often have their jarring interests and opinions deluged with Christian blood this long devoted isle.

'Some thirty years ago our unhappy fathers — galled beyond human sufferance — like a captive lion vainly struggling in the toils, strove violently to snap their bonds asunder, but instead rivetted them more tight. Exhausted by the bloody struggle, the poor of this province submitted to their oppressors, and fattened with their vitals each decimating leech.

'The luxurious parson drowned in the riot of his table the bitter groans of those wretches that his proctor fleeced, and the poor remnant of the doctor's rapine was sure to be gleaned by the rapacious priest; but it was blasphemy to complain of him; Heaven, we thought, would wing its lightning to blast the wretch who grudged the Holy Father's share. Thus plundered by either clergy, we had reason to wish for our simple Druids again.

'At last, however, it pleased pitying Heaven to dispel the murky cloud of bigotry that hovered over us so long. Liberality shot her cheering rays, and enlightened the peasant's hovel as well as the splendid hall. O'Leary told us, plain as a friar could, that a God of universal love would not confine His salvation to one sect alone, and the subjects' election was the best title to the crown.

'Thus improved in our religion and our politics . . . we resolve to evince on every occasion the change in our sentiments and hope to succeed in our sincerest attempts. We examined the double cause of our grievances, and debated long how to get them removed, until at length our resolves terminated in this general peaceful remonstrance.

'Humanity, justice and policy enforce our request. Whilst the tithe farmer enjoys the fruit of our labours, agriculture must decrease, and while the griping priest insists on more from the bridegroom than he is worth, population must be retarded.

'Let the legislature befriend us now, and we are theirs for ever. Our sincerity in the warmth of our attachment when once professed was never questioned, and we are bold to say no such imputation will ever fall on the Munster peasantry.

'At a very numerous and peaceable meeting of the delegates of the Munster peasantry, held on Thursday, the 1st day of July, 1786, the following resolutions were unanimously agreed to, viz:

'Resolved — That we will continue to oppose our oppressors by the most justifiable means in our power, either until they are glutted with our blood or until humanity raises her angry voice in the councils of the nation to protect the toiling peasant and lighten his burden.

'Resolved — That the fickleness of the multitude makes it necessary for all and each of us to swear not to pay voluntarily priest or parson more than as follows:

'Potatoes, first crop, 6s per acre; ditto, second crop, 4s; wheat, 4s; barley, 4s; oats, 3s; meadowing, 2s 8d; marriage, 5s; baptism, 1s 6d; each family confession, 2s; Par. Priest's Sun. Mass, 1s; any other, 1s; Extreme Unction, 1s.

'Signed by order,

'WILLIAM O'DRISCOLL,

'General to the Munster Peasantry.'

Chapter Five

GRATTAN'S PARLIAMENT

'Dynasties and thrones are not half so important as workshops, farms and factories. Rather we may say that dynasties and thrones, and even provisional governments, are good for anything exactly in proportion as they secure fair play, justice and freedom to those who labour.' *John Mitchel*, 1848

WE NOW COME to the period of the Volunteers. In this year, 1778, the people of Belfast, alarmed by rumours of intended descents of French privateers, sent to the Irish Secretary of State at Dublin Castle asking for a military force to protect their town. But the English army had long been drafted off to the United States — then rebel American colonies of England — and Ireland was practically denuded of troops. Dublin Castle answered Belfast in the famous letter which stated that the only force available for the North would be 'a troop or two of horse, or part of a company of invalids'.

On receipt of this news the people began arming themselves and publicly organising Volunteer corps throughout the country. In a short time Ireland possessed an army of some 80,000 citizen soldiers, equipped with all the appurtenances of war; drilled, organised, and in every way equal to any force at the command of a regular government. All the expenses of the embodiment of this Volunteer army were paid by subscriptions of private individuals.

As soon as the first alarm of foreign invasion had passed, the Volunteers turned their attention to home affairs and began formulating certain demands for reform — demands which the government was not strong enough to resist. Eventually, after a few years' agitation on the Volunteer side, met by intrigue on the part of the government, the 'patriot' army, led by Grattan and Flood, and supported by the moral(?) pressure of a Volunteer review outside the walls of the Parliament House, succeeded in obtaining from the legislature a temporary abandonment of the claim set up by the English parliament to force laws upon the assembly at College Green. This and the concession of Free Trade (enabling Irish merchants to trade on equal terms with their English rivals) inaugurated what is known in Irish history as Grattan's Parliament.

At the present day our political agitators never tire of telling us with the most painful iteration that the period covered by Grattan's Parliament was a period of unexampled prosperity for Ireland, and that, therefore, we may expect a renewal of this same happy state with a return of our 'native legislature' as they somewhat facetiously style that abortive product of political intrigue — Home Rule.

We might, if we choose, make a point against our political historians by pointing out that prosperity such as they speak of is purely capitalistic prosperity — that is to say, prosperity gauged merely by the *volume* of wealth produced, and entirely ignoring the manner in which the wealth is distributed amongst the workers who produce it. Thus, in a previous article we quoted a manifesto issued by the Munster Peasantry in 1786, in which — four years after Grattan's Parliament had been established — they called upon the legislature to help them, and resolved if such help was not forthcoming — and it was not forthcoming — to 'resist our oppressors until they are glutted with our blood', an expression which would seem to indicate that the 'prosperity' of Grattan's Parliament had not penetrated far into Munster.

In the year 1794 a pamphlet published at 7 Capel Street, Dublin, stated that the average wage of a day labourer in the County Meath reached only 6d per day in summer, and 4d per day in winter;* and in the pages of the **Dublin Journal**, a ministerial organ, and the **Dublin Evening Post**, a supporter of Grattan's party, for the month of April, 1796, there is to be found an advertisement of a

*6d and 4d — sixpence and fourpence in pre-decimal currency — are equivalent to 2½p and roughly 1½p today.

charity sermon to be preached in the Parish Chapel, Meath Street, Dublin, in which advertisement there occurs the statement that in *three streets* of the Parish of St Catherine's 'no less than 2,000 souls had been found in a starving condition.' Evidently 'prosperity' had not much meaning to the people of St Catherine's.

But this is not the ground we mean at present to take up. We will rather admit, for the purpose of our argument, that the Home Rule capitalistic definition of 'prosperity' is the correct one, and that Ireland was prosperous under Grattan's Parliament, but we must emphatically deny that such prosperity was in any but an infinitesimal degree produced by parliament.

Here again the socialist philosophy of history provides the key to the problem — points to the economic development as the true solution. The sudden advance of trade in the period in question was almost solely due to the introduction of mechanical power and the consequent cheapening of manufactured goods. It was the era of the Industrial Revolution when the domestic industries we had inherited from the Middle Ages were finally replaced by the factory system of modern times. The warping frame, invented by Arkwright in 1769; the spinning jenny, patented by Hargreaves in 1770; Crampton's mechanical mule, introduced in 1779; and the application in 1788 of the steam-engine to blast furnaces, all combined to cheapen the cost of production and so to lower the price of goods in the various industries affected.

This brought into the field fresh hosts of customers, and so gave an immense impetus to trade in general in Great Britain as well as in Ireland. Between 1782 and 1804 the cotton trade more than trebled its total output; between 1783 and 1796 the linen trade increased nearly threefold; in the eight years between 1788 and 1796 the iron trade doubled in volume. The latter trade did not long survive this burst of prosperity. The invention of smelting by coal instead of wood in 1750, and the application of steam to blast-furnaces, already spoken of, placed the Irish manufacturer at an enormous disadvantage in dealing with his English rival, but in the halcyon days of brisk trade — between 1780 and 1800 — this was not very acutely felt.

But, when trade once more assumed its normal aspect of keen competition, Irish manufacturers, without a native coal supply and almost entirely dependent on imported English coal, found it impossible to compete with their trade rivals in the sister country who, with abundant supplies of coal at their own door, found it very easy before the days of railways to undersell and ruin the unfortunate Irish. The same fate, and for the same reason, befell the other important Irish trades.

The period marked politically by Grattan's Parliament was a period of commercial inflation due to the introduction of mechanical improvements into the staple industries of the country. As long as such machinery was worked by hand Ireland could hold her place on the markets, but with this application of steam to the service of industry, which began on a small scale in 1785, and the introduction of the power-loom, which first came into general use about 1813, the immense natural advantage of an indigenous coal supply finally settled the contest in favour of English manufacturers.

A native parliament might have hindered the subsequent decay as an alien parliament may have hastened it, but in either case, under capitalistic conditions, the process itself was as inevitable as the economic evolution of which it was one of the most significant signs. How little parliament had to do with it may be gauged by comparing the positions of Ireland and Scotland.

In the year 1799, Mr Foster in the Irish parliament stated that the production of linen was twice as great in Ireland as in Scotland. The actual figures given were for the year 1796 — 23,000,000 yards for Scotland as against 46,705,319 for Ireland. This discrepancy in favour of Ireland he attributed to the native parliament. But by the year 1830, according to McCulloch's Commercial Dictionary, the one port of Dundee in Scotland exported more linen than all Ireland. Both countries had been deprived of self-government. Why had Scottish manufacture advanced whilst that of Ireland had decayed? Because Scotland possessed a native coal supply, and every facility for industrial pursuits which Ireland lacked.

The 'prosperity' of Ireland under Grattan's Parliament was almost as little due to that parliament as the dust caused by the revolutions of the coach-wheel was due to the presence of the fly who, sitting on the coach, viewed the dust, and fancied himself the author thereof. And, therefore, true prosperity cannot be brought to Ireland except by measures somewhat more drastic than that parliament ever imagined.

Chapter Six

CAPITALIST BETRAYAL OF THE IRISH VOLUNTEERS

'Remember still, through good and ill
How vain were prayers and tears,
How vain were words till flashed the swords
Of the Irish Volunteers.' — *Thomas Davie*

THE THEORY THAT the fleeting 'prosperity' of Ireland in the time we refer to was caused by the parliament of Grattan is only useful to its propagators as a prop to their argument that the Legislative Union between Great Britain and Ireland destroyed the trade of the latter country and that, therefore, the repeal of that Union would lead to the re-establishment of Irish manufactures on a paying basis. The fact that the Union placed all Irish manufactures upon an absolutely equal basis legally with the manufactures of England is usually ignored, or worse still, is so perverted in its statement as to leave the impression that the reverse is the case. In fact many thousands of our countrymen still believe that English laws prohibit mining in Ireland after certain minerals, and the manufacture of certain articles.

A moment's reflection should remove such an idea. An English capitalist will cheerfully invest his money in Timbuctoo or China, or Russia, or anywhere that he thinks he can secure a profit, even though it may be in the territory of his mortal enemy. He does not invest his money in order to give employment to his workers, but to make a profit, and hence it would be foolish to expect that he would allow his parliament to make laws prohibiting him from opening mines or factories in Ireland to make a profit out of the Irish workers. And there are not, and have not been since the Union, any such laws.

If the student desires to continue the study of this remarkable controversy in Irish history and to compare this parliamentarian theory of Irish industrial decline with that we have just advanced — the socialist theory outlined in our previous chapter — he has an easy and effective course to pursue in order to bring this matter to the test. Let him single out the most prominent of the exponents of parliamentarianism and propound the following question:

Please explain the process by which the removal of parliament from Dublin to London — a removal absolutely unaccompanied by any legislative interference with Irish industry — prevented the Irish capitalist class from continuing to produce goods for the Irish market?

He will get no logical answer to his question — no answer that any reputable thinker on economic questions would accept for one moment. He will instead undoubtedly be treated to a long emuneration of the number of tradesmen and labourers employed at manufactures in Ireland before the Union, and the number employed at some specific period, 20 or 30 years afterwards. This was the method adopted by Daniel O'Connell, the Liberator, in his first great speech in favour of Repeal of the Union, the speech in which he began his Repeal agitation, and has been slavishly copied and popularised by all his imitators since.

But neither O'Connell nor any of his imitators have ever yet attempted to analyse and explain the process by which those industries were destroyed. The nearest approach to such an explanation ever assayed is the statement that the Union led to absentee landlordism and the withdrawal of the custom of these absentees from Irish manufacturers.

Such an explanation is simply no explanation at all. It is worse than childish. Who would seriously contend that the loss of a few thousand aristocratic clients killed, for instance, the leather industry, once so flourishing in Ireland and now scarcely existent. The district in the city of Dublin which lies between Thomas Street and the South Circular Road was once a busy hive of such men engaged in the tanning of leather and all its allied trades. Now that trade has almost entirely disappeared from this district. Were the members of the Irish parliament and the Irish landlords the only wearers of shoes in Ireland? — the only persons for whose use leather was tanned and manufactured? If not, how did their emigration to England make it impossible for the Irish manufacturer to produce shoes or harness for the millions of people still left in the country after the Union?

The same remark applies to the weavers, once so flourishing a body in the same district, to the woollen trade, to the fishing trade, to the iron trade, to the flour milling trade, and so on down the line. The people of Ireland still wanted these necessaries of life after the Union just as much as before, yet the superficial historian tells us that the Irish manufacturer was unable to cater to their demand and went out of business accordingly. Well, we Irish are credited with being gifted with a strong sense of humour, but one is almost inclined to doubt it in the face of the gravity with which this parliamentary theory has been accepted by the masses of the Irish people.

It surely is an amusing theory when we consider that it implies that the Irish manufacturers were so heartbroken grieving over losing the trade of a few thousand racketeering landlords that they could not continue to make a profit by supplying the wants of the millions of Irish people at their doors. The English and the Scotch, the French and the Belgian manufacturers, miners, merchants, and fishermen could and did wax fat and prosperous by supplying the wants of the Irish commonality, but the Irish manufacturer could not. He had to shut up shop and go to the poorhouse because my Lord Rackrent of Castle Rackrent, and his immediate personal following, had moved to London.

If our parliamentarian historians had not been the most superficial of all recorders of history; if their shallowness had not been so phenomenal that there is no equal to it to be found except in the bigotry and stupidity of their loyalist rivals they might easily have formulated from the same set of facts another theory equally as useful to their cause, and more in consonance with the truth. That other theory may be stated thus:

That the Act of Union was made possible because Irish manufacture was weak, and, consequently, Ireland had not an energetic capitalist class with sufficient public spirit and influence to prevent the Union.

Industrial decline having set in, the Irish capitalist class was not able to combat the influence of the corruption fund of the English government, or to create and lead a party strong enough to arrest the demoralisation of Irish public life. This we are certain is the proper statement of the case. Not that the loss of the parliament destroyed Irish manufacture, but that the decline of Irish manufacture, due to causes already outlined, made possible the destruction of the Irish parliament.

Had a strong, enterprising and successful Irish capitalist class been in existence in Ireland a parliamentary reform investing the Irish masses with the suffrage would have been won under the guns of the Volunteers without a drop of blood being shed, and with a parliament elected under such conditions the Act of Union would have been impossible. But the Irish capitalist class used the Volunteers to force commercial reforms from the English government and then, headed by Henry Grattan, forsook and denounced the Volunteers when that body sought by reforming the representative system to make it more responsive to the will of the people, thus to secure in peace what they had won by the threat of violence.

An Ireland controlled by popular suffrage would undoubtedly have sought to save Irish industry while it was yet time by a stringent system of protection, which would have imposed upon goods a tax heavy enough to neutralise the advantages accruing to the foreigner from his coal supply, and such a system might have averted that decline of Irish industry which, as we have already stated, was otherwise inevitable.

But the only hope of realising that Ireland lay then in the armed force of the Volunteers, and as the capitalist class did not feel themselves strong enough as a class to hold the ship of state against the aristocracy on the one hand and the people on the other they felt impelled to choose the only other alternative — viz. to elect to throw in their lot with one or other of the contending parties. They chose to put their trust in the aristocracy, abandoned the populace, and as a result were deserted by the class whom they had trusted, and went down into bankruptcy and slavery with the class they had betrayed.

A brief glance at the record of the Volunteer movement will

illustrate the far-reaching treachery with which the capitalist class of Ireland emulated their aristocratic compatriots who

Sold for place or gold
Their country and their God

but, unlike them, contrived to avoid the odium their acts deserved.

At the inception of this movement Ireland was under the Penal Laws. Against the Roman Catholic, statutes unequalled in ferocity were still upon the statute books.

Those laws, although ostensibly designed to convert Catholics to the Protestant faith, were in reality chiefly aimed at the conversion of Catholic-owned property into Protestant-owned property. The son of a Catholic property holder could dispossess his own father and take possession of his property simply by making affidavit that he, the son, had accepted the Protestant religion. Thenceforth the father would be by law a pensioner upon the son's bounty. The wife of a Catholic could deprive her husband of all control over his property simply by becoming a Protestant.

A Catholic could not own a horse worth more than £5. If he did any Protestant could take his horse from him in the light of day and give him £5 in full payment of all rights in the horse. On the head of a Catholic schoolmaster or a Catholic priest the same price was put as on the head of a wolf. Catholics were eligible to no public office, and were debarred from most of the professions.

In fact the Catholic religion was an illegal institution. Yet it grew and flourished, and incidentally it may be observed it secured a hold upon the affections and in the hearts of the Irish people as rapidly as it lost the same hold in France and Italy, where the Catholic religion was a dominant state institution — a fact worth noting by those Catholics who are clamouring for the endowment of Catholic institutions out of public funds.

It must be remembered by the student, however, that the Penal Laws, although still upon the statute book, had been largely inoperative before the closing quarter of the eighteenth century. This was not due to any clemency on the part of the English government, but was the result of the dislike of those laws felt by the majority of intelligent Irish Protestants. The latter simply refused to take advantage of them even to their personal aggrandisement, and there are very few cases on actual record where the property of Catholics was wrested from them by their Protestant neighbours as a result of the Penal Laws in the generations following the close of the Williamite war. These laws were in fact too horrible to be enforced, and in this matter public opinion was far ahead of legislative enactment. All historians agree upon this point.

Class lines, on the other hand, were far more strictly drawn than religious lines, as they always were in Ireland since the break up of the clan system, and as they are to this day. We have the words of such an eminent authority as Archbishop Whately in this connection which, coming as they do, from the pen of a supporter of the British government and of the Protestant establishment, are doubly valuable as a witness to the fact that Irish politics and divisions turn primarily around questions of property and only nominally around questions of religion. He says:

> Many instances have come to my knowledge of the most furious Orangemen stripping their estates of a Protestant tenantry who had been there for generations and letting their land to Roman Catholics . . . at an advance of a shilling an acre.

These Protestants so evicted, be it remembered, were the men and women whose fathers had saved Ireland for King William and Protestantism as against King James and Catholicity, and the evictions here recorded were the rewards of their fathers' victory and their own fidelity. In addition to this class line on the economic field the political representation of the country was the exclusive property of the upper class.

A majority of the members of the Irish parliament sat as the nomineees of certain members of the aristocracy who owned the estates on which the boroughs they 'represented' were situated. Such boroughs were called 'Pocket Boroughs' from the fact that they were as much under the control of the landed aristocrats as if he carried them in his pocket. In addition to this, throughout the entire island the power of electing members of parliament was the exclusive possession of a privileged few. The great mass of the Catholic and Protestant population were voteless.

This was the situation when the Volunteer movement arose.

There were thus three great political grievances before the Irish public. The English parliament had prohibited Irish trade with Europe and America except through an English port, thus crippling the development of Irish capitalism; representation in the House of Commons in Dublin was denied alike to Protestant and Catholic workers, and to all save a limited few Protestant capitalists, and the nomineees of the aristocracy; and finally all Catholics were suffering under religious disabilities.

As soon as the Volunteers (all of whom were Protestants) had arms in their hands they began to agitate for the removal of all these grievances. On the first all were unanimous, and accordingly when they paraded the streets of Dublin on the day of the assembling of parliament, they hung upon the mouths of their cannon placards bearing the significant words: 'FREE TRADE OR ELSE' — and the implied threat from a united people in arms won their case. Free Trade was granted. And at that moment an Irish Republic could have been won as surely as Free Trade.

But when the rank and file of the Volunteers proceeded to outline their demands for the removal of their remaining political grievances — to demand popular representation in parliament — all their leaders deserted. They had elected aristocrats, glib-tongued lawyers and professional patriots to be their officers, and all the higher ranks betrayed them in their hour of need.

After the granting of Free Trade a Volunteer convention was summoned to meet in Dublin to consider the question of popular representation in parliament. Lord Charlemont, the commander-in-chief of the body, repudiated the convention; his example was followed by all the lesser fry of the aristocratic officers, and finally when it did meet, Henry Grattan, whose political and personal fortunes the Volunteers had made, denounced them in parliament as 'an armed rabble'.

The Convention after some fruitless debate adjourned in confusion, and on a subsequent attempt to convene another Convention the meeting was prohibited by government proclamation and the signers of the call for the assembly were arrested and heavily fined. The government, having made peace in America, with the granting of American independence, had been able to mass troops in Ireland

and prepare to try conclusions with the Volunteers. Its refusal to consider the demand for popular representation was its gauge of battle, and the proclamation of the last attempt at a Convention was the sign of its victory. The Volunteers had, in fact, surrendered without a blow.

The responsibility for this shameful surrender rests entirely upon the Irish capitalist class. Had they stood by the reformers the defection of the aristocracy would have mattered little, indeed it is certain that the radical element must have foreseen and been prepared for that defection. But the act of the merchants in throwing in their lot with the aristocracy could not have been foreseen; it was too shameful an act to be anticipated by any but its perpetrators. It must not be imagined, moreover, that these reactionary elements made no attempt to hide their treason to the cause of freedom.

On the contrary, they were most painstaking in keeping up the appearance of popular sympathies and in endeavouring to divert public attention along other lines than those on which the real issues were staked. There is a delicious passage in the **Life of Henry Grattan**, edited by his son, describing the manner in which the government gained possession of the arms of the various corps of Dublin Volunteers, which presents in itself a picture in microcosm of very many epochs of Irish history and illustrates the salient characteristics of the classes and the part they play in Irish public life.

Dublin is Ireland in miniature; nay, Dublin is Ireland in concentrated essence. All that makes Ireland great or miserable, magnificent or squalid, ideally revolutionary or hopelessly reactionary, grandly unselfish or vilely treacherous, is stronger and more pronounced in Dublin than elsewhere in Ireland. Thus the part played by Dublin in any national crisis is surely to be a metropolitan setting for the role played by the same passions throughout the Irish provinces. Hence the value of the following unconscious contribution to the study of Irish history from the pen of the son of Henry Grattan.

In Dublin there were three divisions of Volunteers — corresponding to the three popular divisions of the 'patriotic' forces. There was the Liberty Corps, recruited exclusively from the working class; the Merchant Corps, composed of the capitalist class, and the Lawyer Corps, the members of the legal fraternity. Henry Grattan,

Jr., telling of the action of the government after the passage of the 'Arms and Gunpowder Bill' requiring the Volunteers to give up their arms to the authorities for safe keeping, says the government 'seized the artillery of the Liberty Corps, made a private arrangement by which it got possession of that belonging to the Merchant Corps; they induced the lawyers to give up theirs, first making a public procession before they were surrendered.'

In other words and plainer language, the government had to use force to seize the arms of the working men, but the capitalists gave up theirs secretly as a result of a private bargain, the terms of which we are not made acquainted with; and the lawyers took theirs through the streets of Dublin in a public parade to maintain the prestige of the legal fraternity in the eyes of the credulous Dublin workers, and then while their throats were still husky from publicly cheering the 'guns of the Volunteers', privately handed those guns over to the enemies of the people.

The working men fought, the capitalists sold out, and the lawyers bluffed.

Then, as ever in Ireland, the fate of the country depended upon the issue of the struggle between the forces of aristocracy and the forces of democracy. The working class in town and the peasantry in the country were enthusiastic over the success of the revolutionary forces in America and France, and were burning with a desire to emulate their deeds in Ireland. But the Irish capitalist class dreaded the people more than they feared the British government, and in the crisis of their country's fate their influence and counsels were withdrawn from the popular side.

Whilst this battle was being fought out with such fatal results to the cause of freedom there was going on elsewhere in Ireland a more spectacular battle over a mock issue. And as is the wont of things in Ireland this sham battle engrosses the greatest amount of attention in Irish history.

We have already alluded to the Henry Flood who made himself conspicuous in the Irish parliament by out-Heroding Herod in his denunciation of the government for failing to hang enough peasants to satisfy him. Mr Henry Grattan we have also introduce to our readers. These two men were the parliamentary leaders of the 'patriot party' in the House of Commons — the 'rival Harries', as the Dublin crowd sarcastically described them. When the threat of the Volunteers compelled the English authorities to formally renounce all its rights to make laws binding the Irish parliament these two patriots quarrelled, and, we are seriously informed by the grave and learned historians, the subject of their quarrel divided all Ireland.

In telling what that subject was we hope our readers will not accuse us of fooling; we are not, although the temptation is almost irresistible. We are soberly stating the historical facts. The grave and learned historians tell us that Grattan and Flood quarrelled because Flood insisted that England should be required to promise that it would never again interfere to make laws governing the Irish parliament, and Grattan insisted that it would be an insult to the honour of England to require any such promise.

As we have said, the grave and learned historians declare that all Ireland took sides in this quarrel, even such a hater of England as John Mitchel in his **History of Ireland** seemingly believes this to be the case. Yet we absolutely refuse to give any credence to the story. We are firmly convinced that while Grattan and Flood were splitting the air with their declamations upon this subject, if an enquirer had gone down into any Irish harvest field and asked the first reaper he met his opinion of the matter, the said reaper would have touched the heart of the question without losing a single swing of his hook. He would have said truly:

> An' sure, what does it matter what England promises? Won't she break her promise, anyway, as soon as it suits her, and she is able to?

It is difficult to believe that either Grattan or Flood could have seriously thought that any promise would bind England, a country which even then was notorious all over the world for broken faith and dishonoured treaties. Today the recital of the facts of this famous controversy looks like a poor attempt at humour, but in view of the tragic setting of the controversy we must say that it bears the same relation to humour that a joke would in a torture chamber. Grattan and Flood in this case were but two skilful actors indulging in oratorical horseplay at the death-bed of the murdered hopes of a people.

Were any other argument, outside of the absurdity of the legal hair-splitting on both sides, needed to prove how little such a sham battle really interested the great mass of the people the record of the two leaders would suffice. Mr Flood was not only known to be an enemy of the oppressed peasantry and a hater of the Catholics — that is to say, of the great mass of the inhabitants of Ireland — but he had also spoken and voted in the Irish parliament in favour of a motion to pay the expenses of an army of 10,000 British soldiers to be sent to put down the Revolution in America, and Mr Grattan on his part accepted a donation of £50,000 from the government for his 'patriotic' services and afterwards in excess of gratitude for this timely aid repaid the government by betraying and denouncing the Volunteers.

On the other great questions of the day they were each occupying an equivocal position, playing fast and loose. For instance:

Mr Flood believed in democracy — amongst Protestants, but opposed religious freedom.

Mr Grattan believed in religious freedom — amongst property owners, but opposed all extension of the suffrage to the working class.

Mr Flood would have given the suffrage to all Protestants, rich or poor, and denied it to all Catholics, rich or poor.

Mr Grattan would have given the vote to every man who owned property, irrespective of religion, and he opposed its extension to any propertyless man. In the Irish House of Commons he bitterly denounced the United Irishmen, of whom we will treat later, for proposing universal suffrage, which he declared would ruin the country and destroy all order.

It will be seen that Mr Grattan was the ideal capitalist statesman; his spirit was the spirit of the bourgeoisie incarnate. He cared more for the interests of property than for human rights or for the supremacy of any religion.

His early bent in that direction is seen in a letter he sent to his friend, a Mr Broome, dated 3 November 1767, and reproduced by his son in the latter's edition of the life and speeches of his father. The letter shows the eminently respectable, anti-revolutionary, religious Mr Henry Grattan to have been, at heart, a free thinker, free lover and epicurean philosopher, who had early understood the wisdom of not allowing these opinions to be known to the common multitude whom he aspired to govern. We extract:

> You and I, in this as most other things, perfectly agree; we think marriage is an artificial, not a natural institution, and imagine women too frail a bark for so long and tempestuous a voyage as that of life . . . I have become an epicurean philosopher; consider this world as our *ne plus ultra*, and happiness as our great object in it . . . Such a subject is too extensive and too dangerous for a letter; in our privacy we shall dwell upon it more copiously.

This, be it noted, is perhaps not the Grattan of the poet Moore's rhapsody, but it is the real Grattan.

Small wonder that the Dublin mob stoned this Grattan on his return from England, on one occasion, after attending parliament in London. His rhetoric and heroics did not deceive them, even if they did bewitch the historians. His dramatic rising from a sick bed to appear before the purchased traitors who sold their votes to carry the Union, in order to appeal to them not to fulfil their bargain, makes indeed a fine tableau for romantic historians to dwell upon, but it was a poor compensation to the common people for the Volunteers insulted and betrayed, and the cause of popular suffrage opposed and misrepresented.

A further and, to our mind, conclusive proof of the manner in which the 'Parliament of '82' was regarded by the real nationalists and progresive thinkers of Ireland is to be found in the extract below from the famous pamphlet written by Theobald Wolfe Tone and published September 1791, entitled 'An Argument on behalf of the Catholics of Ireland'.

It is interesting to recall that this biting characterisation of the 'glorious revolution of 1782' from the pen of the most farseeing Irishman of his day, has been so little to the liking of our historians and journalists that it was rigidly boycotted by them all until the present writer reprinted it in 1897, in Dublin, in a series of ' '98 Readings', containing also many other forgotten and inconvenient documents of the same period. Since then it has several times been republished exactly as we reprinted the extract, but to judge by the manner in which some of our friends still declare they 'stand upon the constitution of '82' it has been published in vain for some people.

Wolfe Tone on Grattan's Parliament

(Extract from the famous pamphlet, 'An Argument on behalf of the Catholics of Ireland', published September 1791.)

'I have said that we have no national government. Before the year 1782 it was not pretended that we had, and it is at least a curious, if not a useful, speculation to examine how we stand in that regard now. And I have little dread of being confuted, when I assert that all we got by what we are pleased to dignify with the name of Revolution was simply the means of doing good according to law, without recurring to the great rule of nature, which is above all positive statutes; whether we have done good or not, why we have omitted to do good is a serious question.

'The pride of the nation, the vanity of individuals concerned, the moderation of some honest men, the corruption of knaves, I know may be alarmed when I assert that the revolution of 1782 was the most bungling, imperfect business that ever threw ridicule on a lofty epithet, by assuming it unworthily. It is not pleasant to any Irishman to make such a concession, but it cannot be helped if truth will have it so. It is much better that we should know and feel our real state, than delude ourselves or be gulled by our enemies with praises which we do not deserve, or imaginary blessings which we do not enjoy.

'I leave to the admirers of that era to vent flowing declamations; it is a fine subject, and peculiarly flattering to my countrymen, many of whom were actors, and almost spectators of it. Be mine the unpleasing task to strip it of its plumage and its tinsel, and show the naked figure. The operation will be severe, but if properly attended to may give us a strong and striking lesson of caution and wisdom.

'The Revolution of 1782 was a revolution which enabled Irishmen to sell at a much higher price their honour, their integrity, and the interests of their country; it was a revolution which, while at one stroke it doubled the value of every borough-monger in the kingdom, left three-fourths of our countrymen slaves as it found them, and the government of Ireland in the base and wicked, and contemptible hands who had spent their lives in degrading and plundering her; nay, some of whom had given their last vote decidedly, though hopelessly against this, our famous revolution.

'Who of the veteran enemies of the country lost his place or his pension? Who was called forth to station or office from the ranks of opposition? Not one. The power remained in the hands of our enemies, again to be exerted for our ruin, with this difference, that formerly we had our distresses, our injuries, and our insults *gratis* at the hands of England; but now we pay very dearly to receive the same with aggravation, through the hands of Irishmen — yet this we boast of and call a Revolution!'

And so we close this chapter on the Volunteers — a chapter of great opportunities lost, of popular confidence betrayed. A few extracts from some versees written at the time in Dublin serve as an epitome of the times, even if they do seem a little bitter.

Who aroused the people?
The rival Harries rose
And pulled each others' nose,
And said they aroused the people.

What did the Volunteers?
They mustered and paraded
Until their laurels faded.
Thus did the Volunteers.

How died the Volunteers?
The death that's fit for slaves,
They slunk into their graves,
Thus died the Volunteers.

Chapter Seven

THE UNITED IRISHMEN

'Our freedom must be had at all hazards. If the men of property will not help us they must fall; we will free ourselves by the aid of that large and respectable class of the community — the men of no property.' — *Theobald Wolfe Tone*

CONTEMPORANEOUSLY WITH the betrayal and fall of the Volunteers, Ireland witnessed the rise and progress of the Society of United Irishmen. This organisation was at first an open, peaceful association, seeking to utilise the ordinary means of political agitation in order to spread its propaganda amongst the masses and so prepare them for the accomplishment of its greater end — viz., the realisation in Ireland of a republic on the lines of that established in France at the Revolution. Afterwards, unable to maintain its public character in face of the severe persecution by the British government of any savouring in the least of a democratic nature, the organisation assumed the veil and methods of secrecy, and in that form attained to such proportions as enabled it to enter into negotiations with the revolutionary Directory of France on the basis of an equal treaty-making national power.

As the result of this secret treaty between revolutionary France and revolutionary Ireland against the common enemy, aristocratic England, various fleets and armies were despatched from the Continent to assist the Irish Republicans, but all of those expeditions were disastrous in their outcome. The first, under the command of Grouchy and Hoche, was dispersed by a storm, some of the ships being compelled to return to France for repairs, and when the remainder, including the greater part of the army, reached Bantry Bay, on the Irish coast, the French commander exhibited to the full all that hesitation, indecision and lack of initiative which he afterwards was to show with equally fatal results to Napoleon on the eve of the battle of Waterloo. Finally, despite the desperate protests of the Irish revolutionaries on board, he weighed anchor and returned to France without striking a blow or landing a corporal's guard. Had he been a man equal to the occasion and landed his expedition, Ireland would almost undoubtedly have been separated from England and become mistress of her own national destinies.

Another expedition, fitted out by the Dutch Republic in alliance with France, was detained by contrary winds in the harbour until the British fleet had time to come upon the scene, and then the Dutch commander chivalrously but foolishly accepted the British challenge to fight, and contending under unequal and adverse conditions, was defeated.

An unauthorised but gallant attempt was made under another French officer, General Humbert, and this actually landed in Ireland, proclaimed the Irish Republic at Killala, in Connaught, armed large numbers of the United Irishmen amongst the inhabitants, and in conjunction with these latter fought and utterly routed a much superior British force at Castlebar, and penetrated far into the country before it was surrounded and compelled to surrender to a force more than ten times its own number. The numbers of the French expedition in this case were insufficient for the purposes of making a stand long enough to permit of the people reaching it and being armed and organised efficiently, and hence its failure.

But had Humbert possessed the numbers commanded by Grouchy, or Grouchy possessed the dash and daring of Humbert, the Irish Republic would have been born, for weal or woe, in 1798. It is a somewhat hackneyed observation, but so true that it compels repetition, that the elements did more for England than her armies. Indeed, whether in conflict with the French expeditionary force of Humbert, with the Presbyterians and Catholics of the United Irish Army under General Munro in the North, or with the insurgent forces of Wicklow, Wexford, Kildare and Dublin, the British army can scarcely be said to have at any time justified its reputation, let alone covered itself with glory.

All the glory was, indeed, on the other side, as was also most of the humanity, and all of the zeal for human freedom. The people were wretchedly armed, totally undrilled, and compelled to act without any systematic plan of campaign, because of the sudden arrest and imprisonment of their leaders. Yet they fought and defeated the British troops on a score of battlefields, despite the fact that the latter were thoroughly disciplined, splendidly armed, and directed like a huge machine from one common centre.

To suppress the insurrection in the counties of Wicklow and Wexford alone required all the efforts of 30,000 soldiers; had the plans of the United Irishmen for a concerted uprising all over the island on a given date not failed, the task of coping with the Republican forces would have been too great for the government to achieve. As it was, the lack of means of communication prevalent in those days made it possible for the insurrection in any one district to be almost fought and lost before news of its course had penetrated into some other parts of the country.

While the forces of republicanism and despotism were thus contending for supremacy upon the land, the victory was being in reality decided for the latter by its superiority upon the sea. The successes of the British fleet alone made it possible to keep the shores of England free of invading enemies, and enable Pitt, the English prime minister, to subsidise and maintain the armies of the allied despots of Europe in their conflict with the forces of freedom and progress throughout the Continent.

In face of this undoubted fact, it is somewhat humiliating to be compelled to record that the overwhelming majority of those serving upon that fleet were Irishmen. But unlike those serving in the British army, the sailors and marines of the navy were there against their own will. During the coercive proceeding of the British government in Ireland, in their attempt to compel the revolutionary movement to explode prematurely, the authorities suspended the Habeas Corpus Act (the guarantee of ordinary legal procedure) and instituted Martial Law and Free Quarters for the Military. Under the latter system the soldiery were forced as boarders upon the civilian population, each family being compelled to provide food and lodging for a certain number. For all attempts at resistance, or all protests arising out of the licentious conduct of the brutal soldiery, or all incautious expressions overheard by them during their unwelcome residence in the houses of the people, the authorities had one great sovereign remedy — viz. transportation on board the British fleet.

Thousands of young men were seized all over the island and marched in chains to the various harbours, from then taken on board the English men-of-war ships, and there compelled to fight for the government that had broken up their homes, ruined their lives and desolated their country.

Whenever any district was suspected of treasonable sympathies it was first put under Martial Law, then every promising young man was seized and thrown into prison on suspicion and without trial, and then those who were not executed or flogged to the point of death were marched on board the fleet. All over Ireland, but especially in Ulster and Leinster during the closing years of the 18th and the opening of the 19th century, the newspapers and private letters of the times are full of records of such proceedings, telling of the vast numbers everywhere sent on board the fleet as a result of the wholesale dragooning of the people.

Great numbers of these were United Irishmen, sworn to an effort to overthrow the despotism under which the people of Ireland suffered, and as a result of their presence on board, every British ship soon became a nest of conspirators. The 'Jack Tars of Old England' were conspiring to destroy the British Empire, and anyone at all acquainted with the facts relative to their treatment by their superiors and the authorities cannot wonder at their acts. The subject is not loved by the jingo historians of the English governing classes, and is consequently usually complacently lied about, but, as a cold matter of fact, the 'wooden walls of England', so beloved of the poets of that country, were in reality veritable floating hells to the poor sailors and marines.

Flogging for the most trivial offences was inflicted upon the unsupported word of the most petty officer; the quarters in which the men were compelled to sleep and eat below decks were of the vilest and most unsanitary conditions; the food was the filthiest, and every seaman had to pay tribute to a greedy quartermaster in order to escape actual starvation, and the whole official life of the ship from the captain down to the youngest midshipman was based upon wealth and rank and breathed hatred and contempt for anything belonging to the lower classes.

Mutinies and attempts at mutiny were consequently of constant occurrence, and, therefore, the forcibly impressed United Irishmen found a fertile field for their operations. In the government records of naval courts martial at that time the charge of 'administering the secret oath of the United Irishmen' is one of the commonest against the accused, and the number of men shot and transported beyond seas for this offence is simply enormous.

English and Scottish sailors were freely sworn into the ranks of the conspirators, and the numbers of those disaffected grew to such an extent that on one occasion — the mutiny of the Nore — the sailors were able to revolt, depose their officers, and take command of the fleet. The wisest heads amongst them, the original United Irishmen, proposed to sail the ships into a French port and turn them over to the French government, and for a time they had great hopes of accomplishing this purpose, but finally they were compelled to accede to a proposal to attempt to win over the sailors on some other ships in the port of London before sailing to France.

This they did, and even threatened to bombard the city; but the delay had enabled the government to rally its loyal ships, and also enabled the 'loyal' slaves still on board the revolting ships to play upon the 'patriotic' feelings of the waverers among the British mutineers by representing to them the probability of their being confined in French prisons instead of welcomed as allies. In the end the admiral and officers, by promising a 'redress of their just grievances', succeeded in winning over a sufficient number on each ship to paralyse any chance of resistance, and the mutiny was quenched. The usual tale of shootings, floggings and transportations followed, but the conditions of life on board ship were long in being altered for the better.

It may be wondered that men forcibly impressed and conspirators against a tyrannical government could fight for that government as did those unfortunates under Nelson, but it must be borne in mind that once on board a war vessel and that vessel brought into action with an enemy in the open sea, there was no possibility of escape or even of co-operation with the enemy; the necessity of self-preservation compelled the rebellious United Irishmen or the discontented mutineers to fight as loyally for the ship as did the soulless slaves amongst whom they found themselves. And being better men, with more manhood, they undoubtedly fought better.

In concluding this brief summary of this aspect of that great democratic upheaval we desire to quote from the **Press**, the organ of the United Irishmen, published in Dublin, the following short news item of the period, which we trust will be found highly illustrative of the times in question, as well as a confirmation of the points we have set forth above:

'ROASTING

'Near Castle Ward, a northern hamlet, a father and son had their heads roasted on their own fire to extort a confession of concealed arms. The cause was that the lock of a gun was found in an old box belonging to the wife of the elder man. It is a fact that the above couple had two sons serving on board the British fleet, one under Lord Bridgport, the other under Lord St Vincent.'

Chapter Eight

THE UNITED IRISHMEN AS DEMOCRATS AND INTERNATIONALISTS

'Och, Paddies, my hearties, have done wid your parties,
    Let min of all creeds and profissions agree,
If Orange and Green, min, no longer were seen, min,
    Och, naboclis, how aisy ould Ireland we'd free.'

—*Jamie Hope*, 1798

AS WE HAVE pointed out elsewhere (in a previous article, 'Erin's Hope, the End and the Means') native Irish civilisation disappeared for all practical purposes with the defeat of the Insurrection of 1641 and the break up of the Kilkenny Confederation. This great insurrection marked the last appearance of the Irish clan system, founded upon common property and a democratic social organisation, as a rival to the politico-social order of capitalist feudalism founded upon the political despotism of the proprietors, and the political and social slavery of the actual producers.

In the course of this insurrection the Anglo-Irish noblemen who held Irish tribelands as their private property under the English feudal system did indeed throw in their lot with the native Irish tribesmen, but the union was never a cordial one, and their presence in the councils of the insurgents was at all times a fruitful source of dissension, treachery and incapacity. Professing to fight for Catholicity, they in reality sought only to conserve their right to the lands they held as a result of previous confiscations from the very men, or the immediate ancestors of the men, by whose side they were fighting. They feared confiscation from the new generation of

Englishmen if the insurrection was defeated, and they feared confiscation at the hands of the insurgent clansmen if the insurrection was successful.

In the vacillation and treachery arising out of this state of mind can be found the only explanation for the defeat of this magnificent movement of the Irish clans, a movement which had attained to such proportions that it held sway over and made laws for the greater part of Ireland, issued its own coinage, had its own fleet and issued letters of marque to foreign privateers, made treaties with foreign nations, and levied taxes for the support of its several armies fighting under its flag.

The fact that it had enrolled under its banner the representatives of two different social systems contained the germs of its undoing. Had it been all feudal it would have succeeded in creating an independent Ireland, albeit with a serf population like that of England at the time; had it been all composed of the ancient septs [clans] it would have crushed the English power and erected a really free Ireland, but as it was but a hybrid composed of both, it had all the faults of both and the strength of neither, and hence went down in disaster. With its destruction, and the following massacres, expropriations and its dispersion of the native Irish, the Irish clans disappear finally from history.

Out of these circumstances certain conditions arose well worthy of the study of every student who would understand modern Irish history.

One condition which thus arose was that the disappearance of the clan as a rallying point for rebellions and possible base of freedom made it impossible thereafter to localise an insurrectionary effort, or to give it a smaller or more circumscribed aim than that of the Irish nation. When before the iron hand of Cromwell the Irish clans went down into the tomb of a common subjection the only possible reappearance of the Irish idea henceforth lay through the gateway of a national resurrection.

And from that day forward the idea of common property was destined to recede into the background as an avowed principle of action, whilst the energies of the nation were engaged in a slow and painful process of assimilating the social system of the conqueror; of absorbing the principles of that political society based upon ownership which had replaced the Irish clan society based upon a common kinship.

Another condition ensuing upon the total disappearance of the Irish social order was the growth and accentuation of class distinction amongst the conquerors. The indubitable fact that from that day forward the ownership of what industries remained in Ireland was left in the hands of the Protestant element, is not to be explained as sophistical anti-Irish historians have striven to explain it, by asserting that it arose from the greater enterprise of Protestants as against Catholics; in reality it was due to the state of social and political outlawry in which the Catholics were henceforth placed by the law of the land.

According to the English Constitution as interpreted for the benefit of Ireland, the Irish Catholics were not presumed to exist, and hence the practical impossibility of industrial enterprise being in their hands, or initiated by them. Thus as the landed property of the Catholic passed into the ownership of the Protestant adventurers, so also the manufacturing business of the nation fell out of the stricken grasp of the hunted and proscribed enemies. Amongst these latter there were two elements — the fanatical Protestant, and the mere adventurer trading on the religious enthusiasm of the former. The latter used the fanaticism of the former in order to disarm, subjugate and rob the common Catholic enemy, and having done so, established themselves as a ruling landed and commercial class, leaving the Protestant soldier to his fate as a tenant or artisan.

Already by the outbreak of the Williamite war in the generation succeeding Cromwell, the industries of the North of Ireland had so far developed that the 'Prentice Boys' of Derry were the dominating factor in determining the attitude of that city towards the contending English kings, and with the close of that war industries developed so quickly in the country as to become a menace to the capitalists of England, who accordingly petitioned the King of England to restrict and fetter their growth, which he accordingly did.

With the passing of this restrictive legislation against Irish industries, Irish capitalism became discontented and disloyal without, as a whole, the power or courage to be revolutionary. It was a re-staging of the ever-recurring drama of English invasion and Anglo-Irish disaffection, with the usual economic background.

We have pointed out in a previous chapter how each generation of English adventurers settling upon the soil as owners resented the coming of the next generation, and that their so-called Irish patriotism was simply inspired by the fear that they should be dispossessed in their turn as they had dispossessed others. What applies to the land-owning 'patriots' applies also to the manufacturers. The Protestant capitalists, with the help of the English, Dutch, and other adventurers, dispossessed the native Catholics and became prosperous; as their commerce grew it became a serious rival to that of England, and accordingly the English capitalists compelled legislation against it, and immediately the erstwhile 'English Garrison in Ireland' became an Irish 'patriot' party.

From time to time many weird and fanciful theories have been evolved to account for the transformation of English settlers of one generation into Irish patriots in the next. We have been told it was the air, or the language, or the religion, or the hospitality, or the lovableness of Ireland, and all the time the naked economic fact, the material reason, was as plain as the alleged reason was mythical and spurious. But there are none so blind as those who will not see, yet the fact remains that since English confiscations of Irish land ceased no Irish landlord body has become patriotic or rebellious, and since English repressive legislation against Irish manufacturers ceased Irish capitalists have remained valuable assets in the scheme of English rule in Ireland.

So it would appear that since the economic reason ceased to operate, the air, and the language, and the religion, and the hospitality, and the lovableness of Ireland have lost all their seductive capacity; all the power to make an Irish patriot out of an English settler of the propertied classes.

With the development of this 'patriotic' policy amongst the Irish manufacturing class there had also developed a more intense and aggressive policy amongst the humbler class of Protestants in town and country. In fact in Ireland at that time there were not only two nations divided into Catholics and non-Catholics, but each of those two nations in turn was divided into other two, the rich and the poor.

The development of industry had drawn large numbers of the Protestant poor from agricultural pursuits into industrial occupations, and the suppression of those latter in the interests of English manufacturers left them both landless and workless. This condition reduced the labourers in town and country to the position of serfs. Fierce competition for farms and for jobs enabled the master class to bend both Protestant and Catholic to its will, and the result was seen in the revolts we have noticed earlier in our history.

The Protestant workman and tenant was learning that the Pope of Rome was a very unreal and shadowy danger compared with the social power of his employer or landlord, and the Catholic tenant was awakened to a perception of the fact that under the new social order the Catholic landlord represented the Mass less than the rent roll. The times were propitious for a union of the two democracies of Ireland. They had travelled from widely different points through the valleys of disillusion and disappointment to meet at last by the unifying waters of a common suffering.

To accomplish this union and make it a living force in the life of the nation, there was required the activity of a revolutionist with statesmanship enough to find a common point upon which the two elements could unite, and some great event dramatic enough in its character to arrest the attention of all and fire them with a common feeling. The first, the man, revolutionist and statesman, was found in the person of Theobald Wolfe Tone, and the second, the event, in the French Revolution.

Wolfe Tone had, although a Protestant, been secretary for the Catholic Committee for some time, and in that capacity had written the pamphlet quoted in a previous chapter, but eventually had become convinced that the time had come for more comprehensive and drastic measures than that committee could possibly initiate even were it willing to do so.

The French Revolution operated alike upon the minds of the Catholic and Protestant democracies to demonstrate this fact and prepare them for the reception of it. The Protestant workers saw in it a revolution of a great Catholic nation, and hence wavered in the belief so insidiously instilled into them that Catholics were willing slaves of despotism; and the Catholics saw in it a great manifestation of popular power — a revolution of the people against the aristocracy, and, therefore, ceased to believe that aristocratic leadership was necessary for their salvation.

Seizing this propitious moment, Tone and his associates proposed the formation of a society of men of every creed for the purpose of securing an equal representation of all the people in parliament.

This was, as Tone's later words and works amply prove, intended solely as a means of unity; knowing well the nature of the times and the political oligarchy in power he realised that such a demand would be resisted with all the power of government, but he wisely calculated that such resistance to a popular demand would tend to make closer and more enduring the union of the democracy irrespective of religion. And that Tone had no illusions about the value of the aristocracy is proven in scores of passages in his autobiography. We quote one, proving alike this point, and also the determining effect of the French Revolution upon the popular mind in Ireland:

> As the Revolution advanced, and as events expanded themselves, the public spirit of Ireland rose with a rapid acceleration. *The fears and animosities of the aristocracy rose in the same or a still higher proportion*. In a little time the French Revolution became a test of every man's political creed, and the nation was fairly divided into two great parties — the aristocrats and democrats (borrowed from France) who have ever since been measuring each other's strength and carrying on a kind of smothered war, which the course of events, it is highly probable, may soon call into energy and action.

It will be thus seen that Tone built up his hopes upon a successful prosecution of a class war, although those who pretend to imitate him today raise up their hands in holy horror at the mere mention of the phrase.

The political wisdom of using a demand for equal representation as a rallying cry for the democracy of Ireland is evidenced by a study of the state of the suffrage at that time. In an Address from the United Irishmen of Dublin to the English Society of the Friends of the People, dated Dublin, 26 October 1792, we find the following description of the state of representation:

> The state of Protestant representation is as follows: Seventeen boroughs have no resident elector; sixteen have but one; ninety have thirteen electors each; ninety persons return for 106 rural boroughs — that is 212 members out of 300 — the whole number; fifty-four members are returned by five noblemen and four bishops; and borough influence has given landlords such power in the counties as make them boroughs also . . . yet the Majesty of the People is still quoted with affected veneration; and if the crown be ostensibly placed in a part of the Protestant portion it is placed in mockery, for it is encircled with thorns.
> With regard to the Catholics, the following is the simple and sorrowful fact: Three millions, every one of whom has an interest in the State, and collectively give it its value, are taxed without being represented, and bound by laws to which they have not given consent.

The above Address, which is signed by Thomas Wright as secretary, contains one sentence which certain socialists and others in Ireland and England might well study to advantage, and is also useful in illustrating the thought of the time. It is as follows:

> As to any union between the two islands, believe us when we assert that *our union rests upon our mutual independence. We shall love each other if we be left to ourselves.* It is the union of mind which ought to bind these nations together.

This, then, was the situation in which the Society of United Irishmen was born. That society was initiated and conducted by men who realised the importance of all those principles of action upon which latter day Irish revolutionaries have turned their backs. Consequently, it was as effective in uniting the democracy of Ireland as the 'patriots' of our day have been in keeping it separated into warring religious factions. It understood that the aristocracy was necessarily hostile to the principle and practice of freedom; it understood that the Irish fight for liberty was but a part of the world-wide upward march of the human race, and hence allied itself with the revolutionists of Great Britain as well as with those of France, and it said little about ancient glories, and much about modern misery.

The Report of the Secret Committee of the House of Lords reprinted in full the Secret Manifesto to the Friends of Freedom in Ireland, circulated throughout the country by Wolfe Tone and his associates, in the month of June 1791, and as this contains the draft of the designs of the revolutuionary association known to history as the Society of United Irishmen, we quote a few passages in support of our contentions, and to show the democratic views of its founders. The manifesto is supposed to have been written by Wolfe Tone in collaboration with Samuel Neilson and others:

> It is by wandering from the few plain and simple principles of political faith that our politics, like our religion, has become preaching not practice; words not works. A society such as this will disclaim those party appellations which seems to pale the human hearts with petty compartments, and parcel out into sects and sections common sense, common honesty, and common weal.
>
> It will not be an aristocracy, affecting the language of patriotism, the rival of despotism for its own sake, not its irreconcilable enemy for the sake of us all. It will not, by views merely retrospective, stop the march of mankind or force them back into the lanes and alleys of our ancestors.
>
> This society is likely to be a means the most powerful for the promotion of a great end. What end? *The Rights of Man in Ireland*. The greatest happiness of the greatest numbers in this island, the inherent and indefeasible claims of every free nation to rest in this nation — the will and the power to be happy to pursue the common weal as an individual pursues his private welfare, and to stand in insulated independence, an imperatorial people.
>
> The greatest happiness of the Greatest Number. On the rock of this principle let this society rest; by this let it judge and determine every political question, and whatever is necessary for this end let it not be accounted hazardous, but rather our interest, our duty, our glory and our common religion. The Rights of Man are the Rights of God, and to vindicate the one is

to maintain the other. We must be free in order to serve Him whose service is perfect freedom.

The external business of this society will be — first, publication, in order to propagate their principles and effectuate their ends. Second, communications with the different towns to be assiduously kept up and every exertion used to accomplish a National Convention of the People of Ireland, who may profit by past errors and by many unexpected circumstances which have happened since this last meeting. Third, communications with similar societies abroad — as the Jacobin Club of Paris, the Revolutionary Society in England, the Committee for Reform in Scotland. *Let the nations go abreast.* Let the interchange of sentiments among mankind concerning the Rights of man be as immediate as possible.

When the aristocracy come forward, the people fall backward; when the people come forward, the aristocracy, fearful of being left behind, insinuate themselves into our ranks and rise into timid leaders or treacherous auxiliaries. They mean to make us their instruments; let us rather make them our instruments. One of the two must happen. The people must serve the party, or the party must emerge in the mightiness of the people, and Hercules will then lean upon his club. On the 14th of July, the day which shall ever commemorate the French Revolution, let this society pour out their first libation to European liberty, eventually the liberty of the world, and with their hands joined in each other, and their eyes raised to Heaven, in His presence, who breathed into them an ever-living soul, let them swear to maintain the rights and prerogatives of Ireland as an independent people.

'*Dieu et mon Droit*' (God and my right) is the motto of kings. '*Dieu et la liberté*' (God and liberty), exclaimed Voltaire when he beheld Franklin, his fellow citizen of the world. '*Dieu et nos droits*' (God and our rights), let every Irishman cry aloud to each other the cry of mercy, of justice, and of victory.

It would be hard to find in modern socialist literature anything more broadly International in its scope and aims, more definitely of a class character in its methods, or more avowedly democratic in its nature than this manifesto, yet although it reveals the inspiration and methods of a revolutionist acknowledged to be the most successful organiser of revolt in Ireland since the days of Rory O'More,* all his present-day professed followers constantly trample upon and repudiate every one of these principles and reject them as a possible guide to their political activity. The Irish Socialist alone is in line with the thought of this revolutionary apostle of the United Irishmen.

The above quoted manifesto was circulated in June 1791, and in July of the same year the townspeople and volunteer societies of Belfast met to celebrate the anniversary of the Fall of the Bastille, a celebration recommended by the framer of the manifesto as a means of educating and uniting the real people of Ireland — the producers. From the Dublin **Chronicle** of the time we quoted the following passages from the 'Declaration of the Volunteers and Inhabitants at Large of the town and neighbourhood of Belfast on the subject of the French Revolution'. As Belfast was then the hot-bed of revolutionary ideas in Ireland, and became the seat of the first society of United Irishmen, and as all the other branches of the society were founded upon this original, it will repay to study the sentiments here expressed.

> Colonel Sherman, President:
> Neither on marble, nor brass, can the rights and duties of men be so durably registered as on their memories and on their hearts. We therefore meet this day to commemorate the French Revolution, that the remembrance of this great event may sink deeply into our hearts, warmed not merely with the fellow feeling of townsmen, but with a sympathy which binds us to the human race in a brotherhood of interest, of duty and affection. Here then we take our stand, and if we be asked what the French Revolution is to us, we answer, much. Much as men. It is good for human nature that the grass grows where the Bastille

*Rory O'More was an Irish chieftain and leader of a rebellion in County Offaly in the 1640s.

stood. We do rejoice at an event that means the breaking up of civil and religious bondage, when we behold this mis-shapen pile of abuses, cemented merely by custom, and raised upon the ignorance of a prostrate people, tottering to its base, to the very level of equal liberty and commonwealth. We do really rejoice in this resurrection of human nature, and we congratulate our brother man coming forth from the vaults of ingenious torture and from the cave of death.

We do congratulate the Christian world that there is in it one great nation which has renounced all ideas of conquest, and has published in the first glorious manifesto of humanity, of union, and of peace. In return we pray to God that peace may rest in their land, and that it may never be in power of royalty, nobility, or a priesthood to disturb the harmony of a good people, consulting about those laws which must ensure their own happiness and that of unborn millions.

Go on, then — great and gallant people — to practise the sublime philosophy of your legislation, to force applause from nations least disposed to do you justice, and not by conquest, but by the omnipotence of reason to convert and liberate the world — a world whose eyes are fixed on you, whose heart is with you, who talks of you with all her tongues; you are in very truth the hope of this world, of all except a few men in a few cabinets who thought the human race belonged to them, not them to the human race; but now are taught by awful example, and tremble, and dare not confide in armies arrayed against you and your cause.

Thus spoke Belfast. It will be seen that the ideas of the publishers of the secret manifesto were striking a responsive chord in the hearts of the people. A series of meetings of the Dublin Volunteer Corps were held in October of the same year, ostensibly to denounce a government proclamation offering a reward for the apprehension of Catholics under arms, but in reality to discuss the political situation. The nature of the conclusions arrived at may be judged by a final paragraph in the resolution, passed 23 October 1791, and signed amongst others by James Napper Tandy, on behalf of the Liberty Corps of Artillery. It read:

> While we admire the philanthropy of that great and enlightened nation, who have set an example to mankind, both of political and religious wisdom, we cannot but lament that distinction, injurious to both, have too long disgraced the name of Irishmen; and we most fervently wish that our animosities were entombed with the bones of our ancestors; and that we and our Roman Catholic brethren would unite like citizens, *and claim the Rights of Man.*

This was in October. In the same month Wolfe Tone went to Belfast on the invitation of one of the advanced Volunteer Clubs, and formed the first club of United Irishmen. Returning to Dublin he organised another. From the minutes of the Inauguration Meeting of this First Dublin Society of United Irishmen, held at the Eagle Inn, Eustace Street, 9 November 1791, we make the following extracts, which speak for the principles of the original members of those two parent clubs of a society destined in a short time to cover all Ireland, and to set in motion the fleets of two foreign auxiliaries.

> For the attainment then of this great and important object — the removal of absurd and ruinous distinctions — and for promoting a complete coalition of the people, a club has been formed composed of all religious persuasions who have adopted for their name The Society of United Irishmen of Dublin, and have taken as their declaration that of a similar society in Belfast, which is as follows:
> In the present great era of reform when unjust governments are falling in every quarter of Europe, when religious persecution is compelled to abjure her tyranny over conscience; *when the Rights of Man are ascertained in Theory and that Theory substantiated by Practice*; when antiquity can no longer defend absurd and oppressive forms against the common sense and common interests of mankind; when all government is acknowledged to originate from the people, and to be so far only obligatory as it protects their rights and promotes their welfare; we think it our duty as Irishmen to come forward and state what we feel to be our heavy grievance, and what we know to be its effectual remedy.

> We have no national government; we are ruled by Englishmen and the servants of Englishmen, whose object is the interest of another country; whose instrument is corruption; whose strength is the weakness of Ireland; and these men have the whole of the power and patronage of the country as means to seduce and subdue the honesty and the spirit of her representatives in the legislature. Such an extrinsic power, acting with uniform force in a direction too frequently opposite to the true line of our obvious interests, can be resisted with effect solely by unanimity, decision, and spirit in the people, qualities which may be exerted most legally, constitutionally, and efficaciously by that great measure essential to the prosperity and freedom of Ireland — an equal representation of all the people in parliament . . .
>
> We have gone to what we conceive to be the root of the evil; we have stated what we conceive to be the remedy — with a parliament thus reformed everything is easy; without it nothing can be done.

Here we have a plan of campaign indicated on the lines of those afterwards followed so successfully by the socialists of Europe — a revolutionary party openly declaring their revolutionary sympathies but limiting their first demand to a popular measure such as would enfranchise the masses upon whose support their ultimate success must rest. No one can read the manifesto we have just quoted without realising that these men aimed at nothing less than a social and political revolution such as had been accomplished in France, or even greater, because the French Revolution did not enfranchise all the people, but made a distinction between active and passive citizens, taxpayers and non-taxpayers.

Nor yet can an impartial student fail to realise that it was just this daring aim that was the secret of their success as organisers, as it is the secret of the political effectiveness of the socialists of our day. Nothing less would have succeeded in causing Protestant and Catholic masses to shake hands over the bloody chasm of religious hatreds, nothing less will accomplish the same result in our day among the Irish workers. It must be related to the credit of the leaders of the United Irishmen that they remained true to their principles even when moderation might have secured a mitigation of their lot. When examined before the Secret Committee of the House of Lords at the prison of Fort George, Scotland, Thomas Addis Emmet did not hesitate to tell his inquisitors that if successful they would have inaugurated a very different social system than that which then prevailed.

Few moments in history have been more consistently misrepresented by open enemies and professed admirers than that of the United Irishmen. The *suggestio falsi*, and the *suppressio veri* have been remorselessly used. The middle class 'patriotic' historians, orators, and journalists of Ireland have ever vied with one another in enthusiastic descriptions of their military exploits on land and sea, their hairbreadth escapes and heroic martyrdom, but have resolutely suppressed or distorted their writings, songs and manifestoes. We have striven to reverse the process, to give publicity to their literature, believing that this literature reveals the men better than any partisan biographer can do. Dr Madden, a most painstaking and conscientious biographer, declared in his volume of **The Literary Remains of the United Irishmen**, that he has suppressed many of their productions because of their 'trashy' republican and irreligious tendencies.

This is to be regretted, as it places upon other biographers and historians the trouble (a thousand times more difficult now) of searching for anew and re-collecting the literary material from which to build a proper appreciation of the work of those pioneers of democracy in Ireland. And as Irish men and women progress to a truer appreciation of correct social and political principles, perhaps it would be found possible to say, without being in the least degree blasphemous or irreverent, that the stones rejected by the builders of the past have become the corner-stones of the edifice.

Chapter Nine

THE EMMET CONSPIRACY

'The Rich always betray the Poor.'—*Henry Joy McCracken's* Letter to his sister, 1798.

THE EMMET CONSPIRACY — the aftermath of the United Irish movement of 1798, was even more distinctly democratic, international and popular in its sympathies and affiliations than the latter. The treacherous betrayal of the United Irish chiefs into the hands of the government had removed from the scene of action practically all the middle class supporters of the revolutionary movement and left the rank and file to their own resources and to consult their own inclinations. It was accordingly with these humble workers in town and country Emmet had to deal when he essayed to reorganise the scattered forces of freedom for a fresh grapple with the despotic power of the class government then ruling Ireland and England.

All students who have investigated the matter are as one in conceding that Emmet's conspiracy was more of a working class character than its predecessors. Indeed it is a remarkable fact that this conspiracy, widespread throughout Ireland, England and France, should have progressed so rapidly, and with such elaborate preparations for armed revolt, amongst the poorer section of the populace right up to within a short time of the date for the projected rising, without the alert English government or its Irish Executive being able to inform themselves of the matter.

Probably the proletarian character of the movement — the fact that it was recruited principally amongst the working class of Dublin and other large centres, as well as amongst the labouring element of the country districts, was the real reason why it was not so prolific of traitors as its forerunner. After the conspiracy had fallen through, the government, of course, pretended that it had known of it all along — indeed the British government in Ireland always pretended to be omniscient — but nothing developed during the trial of Emmet to justify such a claim. Nor has anything developed since, although searchers of the government documents of the time, the Castlereagh papers, the records of the secret service and other sources of information have been able to reveal in their true colours of infamy many who had posed in the limelight for more than a generation as wholesouled patriots and reformers.

Thus Leonard McNally, barrister-at-law, and legal defender of the United Irishmen, who acted for all the chiefs of that body at trials, was one of the Catholic Committee and elected as Catholic delegate to England in 1811, looked up to and revered as a fearless advocate of Catholic rights, and champion of persecuted nationalists, was discovered to have been all the time in the pay of the government, acting the loathsome part of an informer, and systematically betraying to the government the inmost secrets of the men whose cause he was pretending to champion in the court-room. But this secret was kept for half a century. Francis Magan, another worthy, received a secret pension of £200 per year from the government for the betrayal of the hiding-place of Lord Edward Fitzgerald, and lived and died revered as an honest, unoffending citizen.

A body of the Royal Meath Militia stationed at Mallow, County Cork, had conspired to seize the artillery stationed there, and with that valuable arm join the insurgents in a body. One of their number mentioned the plot in his confession to the Rev. Thomas Barry, parish priest of Mallow, and was by him ordered to reveal it to the military authorities. The leader of the plotters, Sergeant Beatty, seeing by the precautions suddenly taken that the plot was discovered, fought his way out of the barracks with nineteen men, but was subsequently captured and hanged in Dublin. Father Barry (how ironical the title sounds) received £100 per year pension from the government, and drew this blood-money in secret for a lifetime before his crime was discovered.

It is recorded that the great Daniel O'Connell himself, as a member of the lawyers' Yeomanry Corps of Dublin, was turned out on duty to serve against the rebels on the night of Emmet's insurrection, and in Daunt's 'Recollections' he relates that O'Connell pointed out to him a house in James's Street which he (O'Connell) had searched for 'Croppies' (patriots).

The present writer has seen in Derrynane, O'Connell's ancestral home in County Kerry, a brass-mounted blunderbuss, which we were assured by a member of the family was procured at a house in James's Street, Dublin, by O'Connell from the owner, a follower of Emmet, a remark that recalled to our mind that 'search for Croppies' of which Daunt speaks, and gave rise to a conjecture that possibly the blunderbuss in question owed its presence in Derrynane to that memorable raid.

But although latter-day investigators have brought to the light of day many such treasons against their liberty as those recorded, and have revealed depths of corruption in quarters long unsuspected, nothing has yet been demonstrated to dim the glory or sully the name of the men and women of the working class who carried the dangerous secret of Emmet's conspiracy and guarded it so well and faithfully to the end.

It must be remembered in this connection that at that period the open organisation of labourers for any purpose was against the law, that consequently the trade unions which then flourished amongst the working class were all illegal organisations whose members were in constant danger of arrest and transportation for the crime of organising, and that, therefore, a proposal to subvert the oppressive governing class and establish a republic founded upon the votes of all citizens, as Emmet planned, was one likely to appeal alike to the material requirements and imagination of the Irish toilers. And as they were already trained to secrecy in organisation they naturally made splendid material for the revolutionary movement.

It is significant that the only serious fight on the night of the ill-fated insurrection took place in the Coombe district of the Liberties of Dublin, a quarter inhabited exclusively by weavers, tanners, and shoemakers, the best organised trades in the city, and that a force of Wicklow men brought into Dublin by Michael Dwyer, the insurgent chieftain, were sheltered on the quays amongst the dock labourers and eventually enabled to return home without any traitor betraying their whereabouts to the numerous government spies overrunning the city.

The ripeness of the labouring element in the country at large for any movement that held out hopes of social emancipation may be gauged by the fact that a partial rebellion had already taken place in 1802 in Limerick, Waterford, and Tipperary, where, according to Haverty's **History of Ireland**, the alleged grounds for rebellion were 'the dearness of the potatoes', and 'the right of the old tenants to retain possession of their farms'.

Such were the domestic materials upon which the conspiracy of Emmet rested — working class elements fired with the hope of political and social emancipation. Abroad he sought alliance with the French Republic — the incarnation of the political, social, and religious unrest and revolution of the age, and in Great Britain he formed alliance with the 'Sassenach' reformers who were conspiring to overthrow the English monarchy.

On 13 November 1802, one Colonel Despard, with nineteen others, was arrested in London charged with the crime of high treason; they were tried on the charge of conspiracy to murder the King; although no evidence in support of such a charge was forthcoming. Despard and seven others were hanged. According to the Castlereagh papers, Emmet and Despard were preparing for a simultaneous uprising, a certain William Dowdall, of Dublin, described as one of the most determined of the society of United Irishmen, being the confidential agent who acted for both. Mr W J Fitzpatrick in his books **Secret Service Under Pitt** and **The Sham Squire**, brings out many of these facts as a result of an extensive and scholarly investigation of government records and the papers of private families, yet, although these books were published half a century ago, every recurring Emmet anniversary continues to bring up its crop of orators who know all about Emmet's martyrdom, and nothing about his principles. Even some of the more sympathetic of his panegyrists do not seem to realise that they dim his glory when they represent him as the victim of a protest against an injustice local to Ireland instead of an an Irish apostle of a world-wide movement for liberty, equality and fraternity.

Yet this latter was indeed the character and position of Emmet, and as such the democracy of the future will revere him. He fully shared in the international sympathies of that Dublin Society of United Irishmen who had elected a Scottish reformer to be a United Irishman upon hearing that the government had sentenced him to transportation for attending a reform convention in Edinburgh. He believed in the brotherhood of the oppressed and in the community of free nations, and died for his ideal.

Emmet is the most idolised, the most universally praised of all Irish martyrs; it is, therefore, worthy of note that in the proclamation he drew up to be issued in the name of the 'Provisional Government of Ireland' the first article decrees the wholesale confiscation of church property and the nationalising of the same, and the second and third decrees forbid and declare void the transfer of all landed property, bonds, debentures, and public securities until the national government is established and the national will upon them is declared.

Two things are thus established — viz., that Emmet believed the 'national will' was superior to property rights and could abolish them at will; and also that he realised that the producing classes could not be expected to rally to the revolution unless given to understand that it meant their freedom from social as well as from political bondage.

Chapter Ten

THE FIRST IRISH SOCIALIST: A FORERUNNER OF MARX

'It is a system which in its least repulsive aspects compels thousands and tens of thousands to fret and toil, to live and die in hunger and rags and wretchedness in order that a few idle drones may revel in ease and luxury.' — *Irish People*, 9 July 1864.

FOR IRELAND, as for every other part of Europe, the first quarter of the nineteenth century was a period of political darkness, or unbridled despotism and reaction. The fear engendered in the heart of the ruling classes by the French Revolution had given birth to an almost insane hatred of reform, coupled with a wolfish ferocity in hunting down even the mildest reformers. The triumph of the allied sovereigns over Napoleon was followed by a perfect saturnalia of despotism all over Europe, and every form of popular organisation was ruthlessly suppressed or driven under the surface.

But driving organisations under the surface does not remove the causes of discontent, and consequently, we find that as rapidly as reaction triumphed above ground its antagonists spread their secret conspiracies underneath. The popular discontent was further increased by the fact that the return home of the soldiers disbanded from the Napoleonic wars had a serious economic effect. It deprived the agriculturalists of a market for their produce, and produced a great agricultural and industrial crisis. It threw out of employment all the ships employed in provisioning the troops, all the trades required to build, equip and repair them, all the industries engaged in making war material, and in addition to suspending the work and flooding the labour market with the men and women thus disemployed, it cast adrift scores of thousands of able-bodied soldiers and sailors to compete with the civilian workers who had fed, clothed and maintained them during the war.

In Ireland, especially, the results were disastrous owing to the inordinately large proportion of Irish amongst the disbanded soldiers and sailors. Those returning home found the labour market glutted with unemployed in the cities, and in the rural districts the landlords engaged in a fierce war of extermination with their tenantry, who, having lost their war market and war prices, were unable to meet the increasing exaction of the owners of the soil.

It was at this period the great Ribbon conspiracy took hold upon the Irish labourer in the rural districts, and although the full truth relative to that movement has never yet been unearthed sufficient is known to indicate that it was in effect a secret agricultural trades union of labourers and cottier farmers — a trades union which undertook in its own wild way to execute justice upon the evictor, and vengeance upon the traitor to his fellows.

Also at this time Irish trade unionism, although secret and illegal, attained to its maximum of strength and compact organisation. In 1824 the chief constable of Dublin, testifying before a committee of the House of Commons, declared that the trades of Dublin were perfectly organised, and many of the employers were already beginning to complain of the 'tyranny of the Irish trades unions'.

Under such circumstances it it not to be wondered at that the attention which in the eighteenth century had been given to political reforms and the philosophy thereof gave way in the nineteenth to solicitude for social amelioration.

In England, France and Germany a crop of social philosophers sprang up, each with his scheme of a perfect social order, each with a plan by which the regeneration of society could be accomplished and poverty and all its attendant evils abolished. For the most part these theorists had no complaint to make against the beneficiaries of the social system of the day; their complaint was against the results of the social system. Indeed they in most cases believed that the governing and possessing classes would themselves voluntarily renounce their privileges and property and initiate the new order once they were convinced of its advantages. With this belief it was natural that the chief direction taken by their criticism of society should be towards an analysis of the effects of competition upon buyer and seller, and that the relation of the labourer as producer to the proprietor as appropriator of the thing produced should occupy no part of their examination.

One result of this one-sided view of social relations necessarily was a complete ignoring of historical developments as a factor in hastening the attainment of their ideal; since the new order was to be introduced by the governing class it followed that the stronger that class became the easier would be the transition, and, consequently, everything which would tend to weaken the social bond by accentuating class distinction, or impairing the feelings of reverence held by the labourer for his masters would be a hindrance to progress.

Those philosophers formed socialist sects, and it is known that their followers, when they lost the inspiring genius of their leaders degenerated into reactionaries of the most pronounced type, opposed to every forward move of labour.

The Irish are not philosophers as a rule, they proceed too rapidly from thought to action.

Hence it is not to be wondered at that the same period which produced the Utopian Socialists before alluded to in France, England and Germany produced in Ireland an economist more thoroughly socialist in the modern sense than any of his contemporaries — William Thompson, of Clonkeen, Roscarberry, County Cork — a socialist who did not hesitate to direct attention to the political and social subjection of labour as the worst evil of society, nor to depict with a merciless fidelity to truth the disastrous consequences to political freedom of the presence in society of a wealthy class.

Thompson was a believer in the possibility of realising socialism by forming co-operative colonies on the lines of those advocated by Robert Owen, and to that extent may be classed as a Utopian. On the other hand he believed that such colonies must be built by the labourers themselves, and not by the governing class. He taught that the wealth of the ruling class was derived from the plunder of labour, and he advocated as a necessary preliminary to socialism the conquest of political representation on the basis of the adult suffrage of both sexes. He did not believe in the state as a basis of socialist society, but he insisted upon the necessity of using political weapons to destroy all class privileges founded in law, and to clear the ground of all obstacles which the governing class might desire to put in the way of the growth of socialist communities.

Lest it may be thought that we are exaggerating the merits of Thompson's work as an original thinker, a pioneer of socialist thought superior to any of the Utopian Socialists of the Continent, and long ante-dating Karl Marx in his insistence upon the subjection of labour as the cause of all social misery, modern crime and political dependence, as well as in his searching analysis of the true definition of capital, we will quote a passage from his most important work, published in 1824: 'An Inquiry into the principles of the distribution of Wealth most conductive to Human Happiness as applied to the newly proposed System of the Voluntary Equality of Wealth'. Third edition.

> What, then, is the most accurate idea of capital? It is that portion of the product of labour which, whether of a permanent nature or not, is capable of being made the instrument of profit. Such seem to be the real circumstances which mark out one portion of the products of labour as capital. On such distinctions, however, have been founded the insecurity and oppression of the productive labourer — the real parent, under the guidance of knowledge, of all wealth — and the enormous usurpation over the productive forces and their fellow-creatures of those who, under the name of capitalists, or landlords, acquired the possession of those accumulated products — the yearly or permanent supply of the community. Hence the opposing claims of the capitalist and the labourer.
>
> The capitalist, getting into his hands, under the reign of insecurity and force, the consumption of many labourers for the coming year, the tools or machinery necessary to make their labour productive, and the dwelling in which they must live, turned them to the best account, and bought labour and its future products with them as cheaply as possible. The greater

the profit of capital, or the more the capitalist made the labourer pay for the advance of his food, the use of the implements or machinery and the occupation of the dwelling, the less of course remained to the labourer for the acquisition of any object of desire.

Or again, see how, whilst advocating political form as a means to an end, he depicts its inefficiency when considered as an end in itself:

> As long as the accumulated capital of society remains in one set of hands, and the productive power of creating wealth remains in another, the accumulated capital will, while the nature of man continues as at present, be made use of to counteract the natural laws of distribution, and to deprive the producers of the use of what their labour has produced. Were it possible to conceive that, under simple representative institutions, any such of the expedients of insecurity should be permitted to remain in existence as would uphold the division of capital and labour, such representative institutions (though all the plunder of political power should cease) would be of little further benefit to the real happiness of mankind, than as affording an easy means for the development of knowledge, and the ultimate abolition of all such expedients. As long as a class of mere capitalists exists society must remain in a diseased state. Whatever plunder is saved from the hand of political power will be levied in another way under the name of profit by capitalists who, while capitalists, must be always law makers.

Thompson advocated free education for all, and went into great detail to prove its feasibility, giving statistics to show that the total cost of such education could be easily borne by Ireland, without unduly increasing the burden of the producers. In this he was three generations ahead of his time — the reform he then advocated being only partially realised in our day. Living in a country in which a small minority imposed a detested religion by force upon a conquered people with the result that a ferocious fanaticism disgraced both sides, he yet had courage and foresight enough to plead for secular education and to the cry of the bigots who then as now, declared that religion would die unless supported by the state, he answered:

> Not only has experience proved that religion can exist without interfering with the natural laws of distribution by violation of security, but it has increased and flourished as during centuries in Ireland and in Greece under and in spite of the forced abstraction of its own resources from its own communicants, to enrich a rival and hated priesthood, or to feed the force that enchained it.

How different was the spirit of the socialism preached by Thompson from the visionary sentimentalism of the Utopians of Continental Europe, or of Owen in his earlier days in England, with their constant appeals to the 'humanity' of the possessing classes, is further illustrated by the following passage which, although lengthy, we make no apology for reproducing. Because of its biting analysis of the attitude of the rich in the various stages of political society, and the lust for power which accompanies extreme wealth, the passage might have been written by a socialist of the twentieth century:

> The unoccupied rich are without any active pursuit; an object in life is wanting to them. The means of gratifying the sense, the imagination even, of sating all wants and caprices they possess. The pleasures of power are still to be attained. It is one of the strongest and most unavoidable propensities of those who have been brought up in indulgence to abhor restraint, to be uneasy under opposition, and therefore to desire power to remove these evils of restraint and opposition. How shall they acquire the power? First by the direct influence of their wealth, and the hopes and fears it engenders; then when these means are exhausted or to make these means more effectual they endeavour everywhere to seize on, to monoplise the powers of government. Where despotism does not exist they endeavour to get entirely into their own hands, or in conjunction with the head of the state, or other bodies, they seize as large a portion as they can of the functions of legislation. Where despotism does not exist, or is modified, they share amongst themselves all the subordinate

departments of government; they monopolise, either directly or indirectly, the command of the armed forces, the offices of judges, priests and all those executive departments which give the most power, require the least trouble and render the largest pecuniary returns. When despotism exists the class of the excessively rich make the best terms they can with the despot, to share his power whether as partners, equals, or mere slaves. If his situation is such as to give them a confidence in their strength, they make terms with the despot, and insist on what they call their rights; if they are weak they gladly crawl to the despot, and appear to glory in their slavishness to him for the sake of the delegated power of making slaves to themselves of the rest of the community. Such do the historians of all nations prove the tendencies of excessive wealth to be.

In the English-speaking world the work of this Irish thinker is practically unknown, but on the Continent of Europe his position has long been established. Besides the work already quoted, he wrote an 'Appeal of one-half of the Human Race — Women — agains the Pretensions of the other half — Men — to retain them in Political and thence in Civil and Domestic Slavery', published in London in 1825. 'Labour Rewarded, the Claims of Labour and Capital Conciliated; or, How to Secure to Labour the Whole Product of its Exertions', published in 1827, and 'Practical Directions for the Speedy and Economical Establishment of Communities', published in London in 1830, are two other known works. He also left behind the manuscript of other books on the same subject, but they have never been published, and their whereabouts is now unknown.

It is told of him that he was for twenty years a vegetarian and total abstainer, and in his will he left the bulk of his fortune to endow the first co-operative community to be established in Ireland, and his body for the purpose of dissection in the interests of science. His relations successfully contested the will on the grounds that 'immoral objects were included in its benefit'.

His position in the development of socialism as a science lies, in our opinion, midway between the Utopianism of the early idealists and the historical materialism of Marx. He anticipated the latter in most of his analyses of the economic system, and foresaw the part that a democratisation of politics must play in clearing the ground of the legal privileges of the professional classes. In a preface to the English translation of the work of one of his German biographers, Anton Menger, the writer, H S Foxwell, says of his contribution to economic science:

> Thompson's fame will not rest upon his advocacy of Owenite co-operation, devoted and public spirited as that was, but upon the fact that *he was the first writer to elevate the question of the just distribution of wealth* to the supreme position it has held in English political economy. Up to his time political economy had been commercial rather than industrial, indeed he finds it necessary to explain the very meaning of the term 'industrial', which, he says, was from the French, no doubt adopted from Saint Simon.

If we were to attempt to estimate the relative achievements of Thompson and Marx we should not hope to do justice to either by putting them in contrast, or by eulogising Thompson in order to belittle Marx, as some Continental critics of the latter seek to do. Rather we should say that the relative position of this Irish genius and of Marx are best comparable to the historical relations of the pre-Darwinian evolutionists to Darwin; as Darwin systematised all the theories of his predecessors and gave a lifetime to the accumulation of the facts required to establish his and their position, so Marx found the true line of economic thought already indicated and brought his genius and encyclopaedic knowledge and research to place it upon an unshakable foundation.

Thompson brushed aside the economic fiction — maintained by the orthodox economists and accepted by the Utopian — that profit was made in exchange, and declared that it was due to the subjection of labour and the resultant appropriation by the capitalists and landlords of the fruits of the labour of others. He does not hesitate to include himself as a beneficiary of monopoly. He declared, in 1827, that for about twelve years he had been 'living on what is called rent, the produce of the labour of others'.

All the theory of the class war is but a deduction from this principle. But although Thompson recognised this class war as a fact, he did not recognise it as a factor, as *the* factor in the evolution of society towards freedom. This was reserved for Marx, and in our opinion is his chief and crowning glory.

While Owen and the Continental socialists were beseeching the favour of kings, parliaments and congresses this Irishman was arraigning the rich, pointing out that lust of power forever followed riches, that 'capitalists, while capitalists, would always be law makers' but that 'as long as a class of mere capitalists exists society must remain in a diseased state'. The fact that the daring Celt who preached this doctrine, arraigning alike the social and political rulers of society and society itself, also vehemently demanded the extension of the suffrage to the whole adult population is surely explanation enough why his writings found no favour with the respectable classes of society, with those same classes who so frequently lionised the leaders of the socialist sects of his day.

In our day another great Irishman, Standish O'Grady, perhaps the greatest *litterateur* in Ireland, has been preaching in the pages of **The Peasant**, Dublin, 1908-9, against capitalist society, and urging the formation of co-operative communities in Ireland as an escape therefrom, and it is curiously significant of how little Irishmen know of the intellectual achievements of their race that O'Grady apparently is entirely unconscious of the work of his great forerunner in that field of endeavour.

It is also curiously significant of the conquest of the Irish mind by English traditions that Irish Nationalists should often be found fighting fiercely against socialism as 'a German idea', although every social conception which we find in the flower of Marx we can also find in the bud in Thompson, twenty-three years before the publication of the **Communist Manifesto**, forty-three years before the issue of **Das Kapital**.

We will conclude this chapter by another citation from the Irish pioneer of revolutionary socialism; we say of revolutionary socialism advisedly, for all the deductions from his teachings lead irresistibly to the revolutionary action of the working class. As according to the socialist philosophy the political demands of the working class movement must at all times depend upon the degree of development of the age and country in which it finds itself, it is apparent that Thompson's theories of action were the highest possible expression of the revolutionary thought of his age.

> The productive labourers, stripped of all capital, of tools, houses, and materials to make their labour productive, toil from want, from the necessity of existence, their remuneration being kept at the lowest compatible figure with the existence of industrious habits . . .
> How shall the wretchedly poor be virtuous? Who cares about them? What character have they to lose? What hold has public opinion on their action? What care they for the delicate pleasures of reputation who are tormented by the gnawings of absolute want? How should they respect the property or rights of others who have none of their own to beget a sympathy for those who suffer for their privation?
> How can they feel for others' woes, for others' passing light complaints, who are tormented by their own substantial miseries? The mere mention of the trivial inconveniences of others insults and excites the indignation instead of calling forth their complacent sympathies. Cut off from the decencies, the comforts, the necessaries of life, want begets ferocity. If they turn round they find many in the same situation with themselves, partaking of their feelings of isolation from kindly sympathies with the happy. They become a public to each other, a public of suffering, of discontent and ignorance; they form a public opinion of their own in contempt of the public opinion of the rich, whom, and their laws, they look upon as the result of force alone.
> From whom are the wretched to learn the principle while they never see the practice of morality? Of respect for the security of others? From their superiors? From the laws? The conduct of their superiors, the operation of those laws have been one practical lesson to them of force, of restraint, of taking away without their consent, without any equivalent the fruits of their labour. Of what avail are morals or principles or commands when opposed, when belied, by example? These can never

supply motives of virtuous conduct. *Motives arise from things, from surroundings, circumstances, not from the idleness of words and empty declamations. Words are only useful to convey and impress a knowledge of these things and circumstances. If those things do not exist words are mere mockery.*

With this bit of economic determinist philosophy — teaching that morality is a thing of social growth, the outcome of things and circumstances — we leave this earliest Irish apostle of the social revolution. Fervent Celtic enthusiasts are fond of claiming, and the researches of our days seem to bear out the claim, that Irish missionaries were the first to rekindle the lamp of learning in Europe, and dispel the intellectual darkness following the downfall of the Roman Empire; may we not also take pride in the fact that an Irishman also was the first to pierce the worse than Egyptian darkness of capitalist barbarism and point out to the toilers the conditions of their enslavement, and the essential pre-requisites of their emancipation?

Chapter Eleven

AN IRISH UTOPIA

'Were the hand of Locke to hold from heaven a scheme of government most perfectly adapted to the nature and capabilities of the Irish nation, it would drop to the ground a mere sounding scroll were there not other means of giving it effect than its intrinsic excellence. All true Irishmen agree in what ought to be done, but how to get it done is the question.' — *Secret Manifesto* (Ireland), 1793.

IN OUR last chapter we pointed out how the close of the Napoleonic wars precipitated a commercial crisis in Great Britain and Ireland, and how in the latter country it also served to intensify the bitterness of the relations existing between landlord and tenant. During the continuation of the wars against Napoleon, agricultural prices had steadily risen owing to the demand by the British government for provisions to supply its huge army and navy. With the rise in prices rents had also risen, but when the close of the war cut off the demand, and prices consequently fell, rents did not fall along with them. A falling market and a stationary or rising rent-roll could have but one result in Ireland — viz., agrarian war.

The landlords insisted upon their 'pound of flesh', and the peasantry organised in secret to terrorise their oppressors and protect themselves.

In the year 1829 a fresh cause of popular misery came as a result of the Act granting Catholic Emancipation. Until that year no Catholic had the right to sit in the English House of Commons, to sit on the Bench as a Judge, or to aspire to any of the higher posts in the civil, military, or naval services. As the culmination of a long fight against this iniquitous 'Protestant Ascendancy', after he had aroused the entire Catholic population to a pitch of frenzy against the injustices inherent in it, the Catholic leader, Daniel O'Connell, presented himself as a candidate for the representation in parliament of the County Clare, declaring that if elected he would refuse to take the oath then required of a Member of Parliament, as it libelled the Catholic religion.

In Ireland at that time open voting prevailed, every elector having to openly declare before the clerks of the election and all others who chose to attend, the name of the candidate for whom he voted. In Ireland at that time also most of the tenants were tenants-at-will, removable at the mere pleasure of the agent or landlord. Hence elections were a combination of farce and tragedy — a farce as far as a means of ascertaining the real wish of the electors were concerned, a tragedy whenever any of the tenants dared to vote against the nominee of the landlord. The suffrage had been extended to all tenants paying an annual rental of forty shillings, irrespective of religious belief, but the terrible power of life and death possessed by the landlord made this suffrage ordinarily useless for popular purposes.

Yet when O'Connell appealed to the Catholic peasantry of Clare to brave the vengeance of their landed tyrants and vote for him in the interests of religious liberty they nobly responded. O'Connell was elected, and as a result Catholic emancipation was soon afterwards achieved. But the ruling classes and the British government took their revenge by coupling with this reform a Bill depriving the smaller tenants of the suffrage, and raising the amount of rent necessary to qualify for a vote to ten pounds.

Up till that time landlords had rather encouraged the growth of population on their estates, as it increased the number of their political adherents, but with the passage of this Act of Parliament this reason ceased to exist and they immediately began the wholesale eviction of their tenantry and the conversion of the arable lands into grazing farms. The Catholic middle, professional and landed class by Catholic emancipation had the way opened to them for all the snug berths in the disposal of the government; the Catholics of the poorer class as a result of the same Act were doomed to extermination to satisfy the vengeance of a foreign government, and an aristocracy whose power had been defied where it knew itself most supreme.

The wholesale eviction of the smaller tenants and the absorption of their farms into huge grazing ranches, thus closing up every avenue of employment to labour, meant death to the agricultural population, and hence the peasantry struck back by every means in their power. They formed lodges of the Secret Ribbon Society, made midnight raids for arms upon the houses of the gentry, assembled at night in large bodies and ploughed up the grass lands, making them useless for grazing purposes, filled up ditches, terrorised graziers into surrendering their ranches, wounded and killed those who had entered the service of graziers or obnoxious landlords, assassinated agents, and sometimes in sheer despair opposed their unarmed bodies to the arms of military.

Civil war of the most sanguinary character was convulsing the country; in May 1831, the Lord Lieutenant of Ireland and a huge military force accompanied by artillery marched through Clare to overawe the people, but as he did not stop evictions, nor provide employment for the labourers whom the establishment of grazing had deprived of their usual employment on the farm, the 'outrages' still continued.

Nor were the professional patriots, or the newly emancipated Catholic rich, any more sympathetic to the unfortunate people. They had opened the way for themselves to place and preferment by using the labourer and cottier-farmer as a lever to overthrow the fortress of religious bigotry and ascendancy, and now when the fight was won they abandoned these poor co-religionists of theirs to the tender mercies of their economic masters.

To the cry of despair welling up from the hearts of the evicted families, crouching in hunger upon the road-side in sight of their ruined homes, to the heartbroken appeal of the labourer permanently disemployed by the destruction of his source of employment; to the wail of famishing women and children the politicians invariably had but one answer — 'Be law abiding, and wait for the Repeal of the Union'. We are not exaggerating. One of the most ardent Repealers and closest friends of Daniel O'Connell, Mr Thomas Steele, had the following manifesto posted up in the market place of Ennis and other parts of Clare, addressed to the desperate labourers and farmers:

> Unless you desist, I denounce you as traitors to the cause of the liberty of Ireland . . . I leave you to the government and the fire and bayonets of the military. Your blood be upon your own souls.

This language of denunciation was uttered to the heroic men and women who had sacrificed their homes, their security, and the hopes of food for their children to win the emancipation from religious tyranny of the well-fed snobs who thus abandoned them. It is difficult to see how a promised Repeal of the Union some time in the future could have been of any use to the starving men of Clare, especially when they knew that their fathers had been starved, evicted and tyrannised over *before* just as they were *after* the Union. At that time, however, it was deemed a highly patriotic act to ascribe all the ills that Irish flesh is heir to the Union. For example, a Mr O'Gorman Mahon, speaking in the House of Commons, London, on 8 February 1831, hinted that the snow storm then covering Ireland was a result of the Legislative Union. He said:

> Did the Hon. Members imagine that they could prevent the unfortunate men who were under five feet of snow from thinking they could better their condition by a Repeal of the Union. It might be said that England had not caused the snow, but the people had snow on them, and they thought that their connection with England had reduced them to the state in which they now were.

Another patriot, destined in after years to don the mantle of an Irish rebel, William Smith O'Brien, at this time, 1830, published a pamphlet advocating emigration as the one remedy for Irish misery.

On the other hand, a Commission appointed by the House of Lords in 1839 to inquire into the causes of the unrest and secret conspiracies amongst the poorer class examined many witnesses in close touch with the life of the peasantry and elicited much interesting testimony tending to prove that the evil was much more deeply rooted than any political scheme of government, and that its real roots were in the social conditions. Thus examined as to the attitude of the labourers towards the Ribbon Association, one witness declared:

> Many look to the Association for protection. They think they have no other protection.
> Question: What are the principal objects they have in view?
> Answer: To keep themselves upon their lands. I have often heard their conversation, when they say:
> 'What good did Emancipation do for us? Are we better clothed or fed, or are our children better clothed and fed? Are we not as naked as we were, and eating dry potatoes when we can get them? Let us notice the farmers to give us better food and better wages, and not give so much to the landlord, and more to the workman; we must not be letting them be turning the poor people off the ground.'

And a Mr Poulett Scroope, MP, declared in one of his writings upon the necessity for a Poor Law: 'The Tithe question, the Church, the Grand Jury laws, the more or fewer Catholics appointed to the Sheriffalty or Magistracy — these are all topics for political agitation among the idle mobs; but the midnight massacre, the daily plunder, the frequent insurrection, the insecurity of life and property throughout agricultural districts of Ireland, these are neither caused by agitation, nor can be put down with agitation.'

It will be thus seen that the opinion of the independent Member of Parliament coincided with that of the revolting labourers as to the relative unimportance to the toilers of Ireland of the subjects when then as now bulked most largely in the minds of politicians.

This was the state of things political and social in Ireland in the year 1831, and as it was in Clare the final effective blow had been struck for religious emancipation so it also was Clare that was destined to see the first effort to discover a peaceful way of achieving that social emancipation, without which all other freedom, religious or political, must ever remain as Dead Sea fruit to the palate of labour.

In 1823 the great English socialist, Robert Owen, visited Ireland and held a number of meetings in the Rotunda, Dublin, for the purpose of explaining the principles of socialism to the people of that city. His audiences were mainly composed of well-to-do inhabitants, as was, indeed, the case universally at that period when socialism was the fad of the rich instead of the faith of the poor. The Duke of Leinster, the Catholic Archbishop Murray, Lord Meath, Lord Cloncurry and others occupied the platform, and as a result of the picture drawn by Owen of the misery then existing, and the attendant insecurity of life and property amongst all classes, and his outline of the possibilities which a system of socialist co-operation could produce, an association styling itself the 'Hibernian Philanthropic Society' was formed to carry out his ideas. A sum of money was subscribed to aid the prospects of the society, a General Brown giving £1,000, Lord Cloncurry £500, Mr Owen himself subscribing £1,000, and £100 being raised from other sources.

The society was short lived and ineffectual, but one of the members, Mr Arthur Vandeleur, an Irish landlord, was so deeply impressed with all he had seen and heard of the possibilities of Owenite Socialism, that in 1831, when crime and outrage in the country had reached its zenith, and the insecurity of life in his own class had been brought home to him by the assassination of the steward of his estate for unfeeling conduct towards the labourers, he resolved to make an effort to establish a socialist colony upon his property at Ralahine, County Clare. For that purpose he invited to Ireland a Mr Craig of Manchester, a follower of Owen, and entrusted him with the task of carrying the project into execution.

Though Mr Craig knew no Irish, and the people of Ralahine, as a rule, knew no English — a state of matters which greatly complicated the work of explanation — an understanding was finally arrived at, and the estate was turned over to an association of the people organised under the title of 'The Ralahine Agricultural and Manufacturing Co-Operative Association'.

In the preamble of the Laws of the Association, its objects were defined as follows:

> The acquisition of a common capital.
> The attainment of a greater share of the comforts of life of poverty, sickness, infirmity, and old age.

The attainment of a greater share of the comforts of life than the working classes now possess.

The mental and moral improvement of its adult members.

The education of their children.

The following paragraphs selected from the Rules of the Association will give a pretty clear idea of its most important features:

'*Basis of the Society*

'That all the stock, implements of husbandry, and other property belong to and are the property of Mr Vandeleur, until the society accumulates sufficient to pay for them; they then become the joint property of the Society.

'*Production*

'We engage that whatever talents we may individually possess, whether mental or muscular, agricultural, manufacturing, or scientific, shall be directed to the benefit of all, as well by their immediate exercise in all necessary occupations as by communicating our knowledge to each other, and particularly to the young.

'That, as far as can be reduced to practice, each individual shall assist in agricultural operations, particularly in harvest, it being fully understood that no individual is to act as steward, but all are to work.

'That the youth, male or female, do engage to learn some useful trade, together with agriculture and gardening, between the ages of nine and seventeen years.

'That the committee meet every evening to arrange the business for the following day.

'That the hours of labour be from six in the morning till six in the evening, in summer, and from daybreak till dusk, in winter, with the intermission of one hour for dinner.

'That each agricultural labouring man shall receive eightpence, and every woman fivepence per day for their labour (these were the ordinary wages of the country, the secretary, storekeeper, smiths, joiners, and a few others received something more; the excess being borne by the proprietors) which it is expected will be paid out at the store in provisions or any other article the society may produce or keep there; any other articles may be purchased elsewhere.

'That no member be expected to perform any service or work but such as is agreeable to his or her feelings, or they are able to perform; but if any member thinks that any other member is not usefully employing his or her time, it is his or her duty to report it to the committee, whose duty it will be to bring that member's conduct before a general meeting, who shall have power, if necessary, to expel that useless member.

'*Distribution and domestic economy*

'That all the services usually performed by servants be performed by the youth of both sexes under the age of seventeen years, either by rotation or choice.

'That the expenses of the children's food, clothing, washing, lodging, and education be paid out of the common funds of the society, from the time they are weaned till they arrive at the age of seventeen, when they shall be eligible to become members.

'That a charge be made for the food and clothing, etc., of those children trained by their parents, and residing in their dwelling-houses.

'That each person occupying a house, or cooking and consuming their victuals therein, must pay for the fuel used.

'That no charge be made for fuel used in the public room.

'That it shall be a special object for the sub-committee of domestic economy, or the superintendent of that department to ascertain and put in practice the best and most economical methods of preparing and cooking the food.

'That all the washing up be done together in the public wash-house; the expenses of soap, labour, fuel, etc., to be equally borne by all the adult members.

'That each member pay the sum of one half-penny out of every shilling received as wages to form a fund to be placed in the hands of the committee, who shall pay the wages out of this fund to any member who may fall sick or meet with an accident.

'Any damage done by a member to the stock, implements, or any other property belonging to the society to be made good out of the wages of the individual, unless the damage is satisfactorily accounted for to the committee.

'Education and formation of character

'We guarantee each other that the young children of any person dying, whilst a member of this society, shall be equally protected, educated and cherished with the children of the living members, and entitled, when they arrive at the age of seventeen, to all the privileges of members.

'That each individual shall enjoy perfect liberty of conscience, and freedom of expression of opinion, and in religious worship.

'That no spirituous liquors of any kind, tobacco, or snuff be kept in the store, or on the premises.

'That if any of us should unfortunately have a dispute with any other person, we agree to abide by a decision of the majority of the members, or any person to whom the matter in question may be by them referred.

'That any person wishing to marry another do sign a declaration to that effect one week previous to the marriage taking place, and that immediate preparations be made for the erection, or fitting up of a suitable dwellinghouse for their reception.

'That any person wishing to marry another person, not a member, shall sign a declaration according to the last rule; the person not a member shall be balloted for, and if rejected, both must leave the society.

'That if the conduct of any member be found injurious to the well-being of the society, the committee shall explain to him or her in what respect his or her conduct has been injurious, and if the said member shall continue to transgress the rules, such member shall be brought before a general meeting, called for the purpose, and if the complaint be substantiated, three-fourths of the members present shall have power to expel, by ballot, such refractory member.

'Government

'The Society to be governed, and its business transacted, by a committee of nine members, to be chosen half-yearly, by ballot, by all the adult male and female members, the ballot list to contain at least four of the last committee.

'The committee to meet every evening, and their transactions to be regularly entered into a minute book, the recapitulation of which is to be given at the society's general meeting by the secretary.

'That there be a general weekly meeting of the society; that the treasurer's accounts be audited by the committee, and read over to the society; that the "Suggestion Book" be also read at this meeting.'

The colony did not use the ordinary currency of the country, but instead adopted a 'Labour Note' system of payment, all workers being paid in notes according to the number of hours worked, and being able to exchange the notes in the store for all the necessities of life. The notes were printed on stiff cardboard about the size of a visiting card, and represented the equivalent of a whole, a half, a quarter, an eighth, and a sixteenth of a day's labour. There were also special notes printed in red ink representing respectively the labours of a day and a half, and two days. In his account of the colony published under the title of **History of Ralahine**, by Heywood and Sons, Manchester (a book we earnestly recommend to all our own readers), Mr Craig says: 'The labour was recorded daily on a "Labour Sheet", which was exposed to view during the following week. The members could work or not at their own discretion. If no work, no record, and, therefore, no pay. Practically the arrangement was of great use. There were no idlers.' Further on he comments:

> The advantages of the labour notes were soon evident in the saving of members. They had no anxiety as to employment, wages, or the price of provisions. Each could partake of as much vegetable food as he or she could desire. The expenses of the children from infancy, for food or education, were provided for out of the common fund.
>
> The object should be to obtain a rule of justice, if we seek the law of righteousness. This can only be fully realised in that equality arising out of a community of property where the labour of one member is valued at the rate of that of another member, and labour is exchanged for labour. It was not possible

to attain to this condition of equality at Ralahine, but we made such arrangements as would impart a feeling of security, fairness and justice to all. The prices of provisions were fixed and uniform. A labourer was charged one shilling a week for as many vegetables and as much fruit as he chose to consume; milk was a penny per quart; beef and mutton fourpence, and pork two and one-half pence per pound. The married members occupying separate quarters were charged sixpence per week for rent, and twopence for fuel.

In dealing with Ireland no one can afford to ignore the question of the attitude of the clergy; it is therefore interesting to quote the words of an English visitor to Ralahine, a Mr Finch, who afterwards wrote a series of fourteen letters describing the community, and offered to lay a special report before a Select Committee of the House of Commons upon the subject. He says:

> The only religion taught by the society was the unceasing practice of promoting the happiness of every man, woman, and child to the utmost extent in their power. Hence the Bible was not used as a school-book; no sectarian opinions were taught in the schools; no public dispute about religious dogmas or party political questions took place; nor were members allowed to ridicule each other's religion; nor were there any attempts at proselytism. Perfect freedom in the performance of religious duties and religious exercises was guaranteed to all. The teaching of religion was left to ministers of religion and to the parents; but no priest or minister received anything from the funds of the society. Nevertheless, both Protestant and Catholic priests were friendly to the system as soon as they understood it, and one reason was they found these sober, industrious persons had now a little to give them out of their earnings, where as formerly they had been beggars.

Mr Craig also states that the members of the community, after it had been in operation for some time, were better Catholics than before they began. He had at first considerable difficulty in warding off the attacks of zealous Protestant proselytisers, and his firmness in doing so was one of the chief factors in winning the confidence of the people as well as their support in insisting upon the absolutely non-sectarian character of the teaching.

All disputes between the members were settled by appeals to a general meeting in which all the adults of both sexes participated, and from which all judges, lawyers, and other members of the legal fraternity were rigorously excluded.

To those who fear that the institution of common property will be inimical to progress and invention, it must be reassuring to learn that this community of 'ignorant' Irish peasants introduced into Ralahine the first reaping machine used in Ireland, and hailed it as a blessing at a time when the gentlemen farmers of England were still gravely debating the practicability of the invention. From an address to the agricultural labourers of the County Clare, issued by the community on the occasion of the introduction of this machine, we take the following passages, illustrative of the difference of effect between invention under common ownership and under capitalist ownership:

> This machine of ours is one of the first machines ever given to the working clases to lighten their labour, and at the same time to increase their comforts. It does not benefit any one person among us exclusively, nor throw any individual out of employment. Any kind of machinery used for shortening labour — except used in a co-operative society like ours — must tend to lessen wages, and to deprive working men of employment, and finally either to starve them, force them into some other employment (and then reduce wages in that also) or compel them to emigrate. Now, if the working classes would cordially and peacefully unite to adopt our system, no power or party could prevent their success.

This was published by order of the committee, 21 August 1833, and when we observe the date we cannot but wonder at the numbers of things Clare — and the rest of Ireland — has forgotten since.

It must not be supposed that the landlord of the estate on which Ralahine was situated had allowed his enthusiasm for socialism to run away with his self-interest. On the contrary, when turning over his farms to the community he stipulated for the payment to himself of a very heavy rental in kind. We extract from **Brotherhood**, a Christian Socialist Journal published in the North of Ireland in 1891, a statement of the rental, and a very luminous summing-up of the lesson of Ralahine, by the editor, Mr Bruce Wallace, long a hard and unselfish worker for the cause of socialism in Ireland:

> The Association was bound to deliver annually, either at Ralahine, Bunratty, Clare, or Limerick, as the landlord might require, free of expense —
> Wheat: 320 brls.
> Barley: 240 brls.
> Oats: 50 brls.
> Butter: 10 cwt.
> Pork: 30 cwt.
> Beef: 70 cwt.
> At the prices then prevailing, this amount of produce would be equivalent to about £900, £700 of rent for the use of natural forces and opportunities, and £200 of interest upon capital. It was thus a pretty stiff tribute that these poor Irish toilers had to pay for the privilege of making a little bit of their native soil fruitful. This tribute was, of course, so much to be deducted from the means of improving their sunken condition. In any future efforts that may be made to profit by the example of Ralahine and to apply again the principles of co-operation in farming, there ought to be the utmost care taken to reduce to a minimum the tribute payable to non-workers, and if possible to get rid of it altogether. If, despite this heavy burden of having to produce a luxurious maintenance for loungers, the condition by the toilers at Ralahine, as we shall see, was marvellously raised by the introduction of the co-operative principle amongst them, how much more satisfactorily would it have been raised had they been free of that depressing dead weight?

Such is the lesson of Ralahine. Had all the land and buildings belonged to the people, had all other estates in Ireland been conducted on the same principles, and the industries of the country also organised, had each of them appointed delegates to confer on the business of the country at some common centre as Dublin, the framework and basis of a free Ireland would have been realised. And when Ireland does emerge into complete control of her own destinies she must seek the happiness of her people in the extension on a national basis of the social arrangements of Ralahine, or else be but another social purgatory for her poor — a purgatory where the pangs of the sufferers will be heightened by remembering the delusive promises of political reformers.

In the most crime-ridden county in Ireland this partial experiment in socialism abolished crime; where the fiercest fight for religious domination had been fought it brought the mildest tolerance; where drunkenness had fed fuel to the darkest passions it established sobriety and gentleness; where poverty and destitution had engendered brutality, midnight marauding, and a contempt for all social bonds, it enthroned security, peace and reverence for justice, and it did this solely by virtue of the influence of the new social conception attendant upon the institution of common property bringing a common interest to all.

Where such changes came in the bud, what might we not expect from the flower? If a partial experiment in socialism, with all its drawbacks of an experiment, will achieve such magnificent results what could we not rightfully look for were all Ireland, all the world, so organised on the basis of common property, and exploitation and mastership forever abolished?

The downfall of the Association came as a result of the iniquitous land laws of Great Britain refusing to recognise the right of such a community to hold a lease or to act as tenants. The landlord, Mr Vandeleur, lost his fortune in a gambling transaction in Dublin, and fled in disgrace unable to pay his debts. The persons who took over the estate under bankruptcy proceedings refused to recognise the community, insisting upon treating its members as common labourers on the estate, seized upon the buildings and grounds and broke up the Association.

So Ralahine ended. But in the rejuvenated Ireland of the future the achievement of those simple peasants will be dwelt upon with admiration as a great and important landmark in the march of the human race towards its complete social emancipation. Ralahine was an Irish point of interrogation erected amidst the wilderness of capitalist thought and feudal practice, challenging both in vain for an answer.

Other smaller communities were also established in Ireland during the same period. A Lord Wallscourt established a somewhat similar community on his estate in County Galway; **The Quarterly Review** of November 1819 states that there was then a small community existent nine miles outside Dublin, which held thirty acres, supported a priest and a school of 300 children, had erected buildings, made and sold jaunting cars, and comprised butchers, carpenters and wheelrights; the Quakers of Dublin established a Co-operative Woollen Factory, which flourished until it was destroyed by litigation set on foot by dissatisfied members who had been won over to the side of rival capitalists, and a communal home was established and long maintained in Dublin by members of the same religious sect, but without any other motive than that of helping forward the march of social amelioration. We understand that the extensive store of Messrs Ganly and Sons on Usher's Quay in Dublin was the home of this community, who lived, worked and enjoyed themselves in the spacious halls, and slept in the smaller rooms of what is now the property of a capitalist auctioneer.

Chapter Twelve

A CHAPTER OF HORRORS: DANIEL O'CONNELL AND THE WORKING CLASS

' 'Tis civilisation, so ye say, and cannot be changed for the weakness of men,
— Take heed, take heed, 'tis a dangerous way to drive the wild wolf to the end of his den,
Take heed of your civilisation, ye, 'tis a pyramid built upon quivering hearts,
There are times, as in Paris in '93, when the commonest men play terrible parts,
Take heed of your progress, its feet are shod with the souls it slew with its own pollutions,
Submission is good, but the order of Good may flame the torch of the revolutions.' —*John Boyle O'Reilly*

FOR BOTH Ireland and Great Britain the period between the winning of Catholic Emancipation (1829) and the year 1850 was marked by great misery and destitution amongst the producing classes, accompanied by abortive attempts at revolution in both countries, and the concession of some few unimportant political and social reforms.

In Ireland the first move against the forces of privilege was the abolition of the tithes, or, more correctly speaking, the abolition of the harsh and brutal features attendant upon the collection of the tithes. The clergy of the Episcopalian Church, the church by law established in Ireland, were legally entitled to levy upon the people of each district, irrespective of religion, a certain tax for the upkeep of that church and its ministers. The fact that this was in conformity with the practice of the Catholic Church in countries where it was dominant did not, of course, make this any more palatable to the Catholic peasantry of Ireland, who continually saw a part of their crops seized upon and sold to maintain a clergy whose ministrations they never attended and whose religion they detested. Eventually their discontent at the injustice grew so acute as to flare forth in open rebellion, and accordingly all over Ireland the tenants began to resist the collection of tithes by every means in their power.

The Episcopalian clergyman called on the aid of the law, and, escorted by police and military, seized the product of the poor tenants and carried them off to be sold at auction; the peasantry, on the other hand, collected at dead of night, and carried off crops and cattle from farms upon which the distraint was to be made, and when that was impossible they strove by acts of violence to terrorise auctioneers and buyers from consummating the sale.

Many a bright young life was extinguished on the gallows or rotted away in prison cells as a result of this attempt to sustain a hated religion by contributions extracted at the point of the bayonet, until eventually the struggle assumed all the aspects of a civil war. At several places when the military were returning from raiding the farms of some poor peasant the country people gathered, erected barricades, and opposed their passage by force. Significantly enough of the temper and qualities of the people in those engagements, they generally succeeded in rescuing their crops and cattle from the police and military, and in demonstrating that Ireland still possessed all the material requisite for armed rebellion.

In one conflict at Newtownbarry twelve peasants were shot and twenty fatally wounded; in another at Carrigshock eleven policemen were killed and seventeen wounded; and at a great fight at Rathcormack, twelve peasants were killed in a fight with a large body of military and armed police. Eye-witnesses declared that the poor farmers and labourers engaged stood the charge and volleys of the soldiers as firmly as if they had been seasoned troops, a fact that impressed the government more than a million speeches would have done.

The gravity of the crisis was enhanced by the contrast between the small sum often involved and the bloodshed necessary to recover it. Thus at Rathcormack the twelve peasants were massacred in an attempt to save the effects of a poor widow from being sold to pay a sum of forty shillings due as tithes.

The ultimate effect of all this resistance was the passage of a 'Tithes Commutation Act' by which the collection of tithes was abolished, and the substitution in its place of a 'Tithe Rent Charge' by means of which the sums necessary for the support of the Episcopalian clergy were included in the rent and paid as part of that tribute to the landed aristocracy. In other words, the economic drain remained, but it was deprived of all the more odious and galling features of its collection.

The secret Ribbon and Whiteboy Societies were the most effective weapons of the peasantry in this fight, and to their activities the victory is largely to be attributed. The politicians gave neither help nor countenance to the fight, and save for the advocacy of one small Dublin newspaper, conducted by a small but brilliant band of young Protestant writers, no journal in all Ireland championed their cause.

For the Catholic clergy it is enough to say that while this tithe war was being waged they were almost universally silent about that 'grievous sin of secret conspiracy' upon which they are usually so eloquent. We would not dare to say that they recognised that as the secret societies were doing their work against a rival priesthood, it was better to be sparing in their denunciations for the time being; perhaps that is not the explanation, but at all events it is noteworthy that as soon as the tithe war was won all the old stock invectives against every kind of extra-constitutional action were renewed.

Contemporaneously with this tithe war had grown up the agitation for repeal of the Legislative Union led by Daniel O'Connell, and supported by the large body of the middle classes, and by practically all the Catholic clergy. At the outset of this agitation the Irish working class, partly because they accepted O'Connell's explanation of the decay of Irish trade as due to the Union, and partly because they did not believe he was sincere in his professions of loyalty to the English monarchy, nor in his desire to limit his aims to repeal, enthusiastically endorsed and assisted his agitation.

He, on his part, incorporated the trade bodies in his association with rights equal to that of regularly enrolled members, a proceeding which evoked considerable dissent from many quarters. Thus the **Irish Monthly Magazine** (Dublin), a rabidly O'Connellite journal, in its issue of September 1832, complains that the National Union (of Repealers) is in danger because 'there is a contemporary union composed of the tradesmen and operative classes, the members of which are qualified to vote at its sittings, and who are in every respect put upon a perfect equality with the members of the National Union'. And in its December number of the same year it returns to the charge with the significant statement that 'In fact we apprehend great mischief and little good from the trades union as at present constituted.'

The representative of the English King in Ireland, Lord Lieutenant Anglesey, apparently coincided in the opinion of this follower of O'Connell as to the danger of Irish trade unions in politics, for when the Dublin trades bodies projected a mammoth demonstration in favour of Repeal, he immediately proclaimed it, and ordered the military to suppress it, if necessary by armed force.

But as O'Connell grew in strength in the country and attracted to himself more and more of the capitalist and professional classes in Ireland, and as he became more necessary to the schemes of the Whig politicians in England, and thought these latter more necessary to his success, he ceased to play for the favour of organised labour, and gradually developed into the most bitter and unscrupulous enemy of trade unionism Ireland has yet produced, singling the trades unions of Dublin out always for his most venomous attacks.

In 1835 O'Connell took his seat on the Ministerial side of the House of Commons as a supporter of the Whig government. At that time the labouring population of England were the most exploited, degraded, and almost dehumanised of all the peoples of Europe. The tale of their condition reveals such inhumanity on the part of their masters, such woeful degradation on the side of the toilers, that were it not attested by the sober record of witnesses before various Parliamentary Commissions the record would be entirely unbelievable.

Women worked down in coal mines almost naked for a pitiful wage, often giving birth to children when surprised by the pains of parturition amidst the darkness and gloom of their places of employment; little boys and girls were employed drawing heavy hutches (wagons) of coal along the pit floors by means of a strap around their bodies and passing through between their little legs; in cotton factories little tots of eight, seven, and even six years of age of both sexes were kept attending machinery, being hired like slaves from workhouses for that purpose, and worked twelve, fourteen, and even sixteen hours per day, living, sleeping, and working under conditions which caused them to die off with a plague; in pottery works, bakeshops, clothing factories and workrooms the overwork and unhealthy conditions of employment led to such suffering and degradation and shortening of life that the very existence of the working class was endangered.

In the agricultural districts the sufferings of the poor were so terrible that the English agricultural labourer — the most stolidly patient, unimaginative person on the face of the earth — broke out into riots, machine breaking, and hay-rick burning. As in Ireland, Captain Rock or Captain Moonlight has been supposed to be the presiding genius of the nocturnal revolts of the peasantry, so in England, Captain Swing, an equally mythical personage, took the blame or the credit. In a booklet circulated amongst the English agricultural labourers, Captain Swing is made to say: 'I am not the author of these burnings. These fires are caused by farmers having been turned out of their lands to make room for foxes, peasants confined two years in prison for picking up a dead partridge, and parsons taking a poor man's only cow for the tithe of his cabbage garden.'

So great was the distress, so brutal the laws, and so hopelessly desperate the labourers that in the Special Assize held in Winchester in December 1830, no less than three hundred prisoners were put on trial, a great number of whom were sentenced to death. Of the number so condemned, six were actually hanged, twenty transported for life, and the rest for smaller periods. We are told in the **English Via Dolorosa**, of William Heath, that 'a child of fourteen had sentence of death recorded against him; and two brothers, one twenty, the other nineteen were ruthlessly hanged on Pendenden Heath, whither they were escorted by a regiment of Scots Greys.'

As to who were responsible for all this suffering, contemporary witnesses leave no doubt. The London **Times**, most conservative of all capitalist papers, in its issue of 27 December 1830, declared: 'We do not affirm that the actions of this pitiable class of men (the labourers) are a commentary on the treatment experienced by them at the hands of the upper and middling classes. The present population must be provided for in body and spirit on more liberal and Christian principles or the whole mass of labourers will start into legions of *banditti* — *banditti* less criminal than those who have made them so, those who by a just but fearful retribution will soon become their victims'. And in 1833 a Parliamentary Commission reported that, 'The condition of the agricultural labourers was brutal and wretched; their children during the day were struggling with the pigs for food, and at night were huddled down on damp straw under a roof of rotten thatch.'

In the large towns the same state of rebellion prevailed, the military were continually on duty, and so many people were killed that the coroners ceased to hold inquests. Such was the state of England — misery and revolt beneath, and sanguinary repression coupled with merciless greed above — at the time when O'Connell, taking his seat in parliament, threw all his force on the side of capitalist privilege and against social reform.

In 1838 five cotton spinners in Glasgow, in Scotland, were sentenced to seven years' transportation for acts they had committed in connection with trade union combination to better the miserable conditions of their class. As the punishment was universally felt to be excessive, even in the brutal spirit of the times, a Mr Walkley, Member of Parliament for Finsbury, on 13 February of that year, brought forward a motion in the House of Commons for a 'Select Committee to inquire into the constitution, practices, and effects of the Association of Cotton Operatives of Glasgow'. O'Connell opposed the motion, and used the opportunity to attack the Irish trade unions. He said:

> There was no tyranny equal to that which was exercised by the trade unionists in Dublin over their fellow labourers. One rule of the workmen prescribed a minimum rate of wages, *so that the best workmen received no more than the worst*. Another part of their system was directed towards depriving the masters of all

freedom in their power of selecting workmen. The names of the workmen being inscribed in a book, and the employer compelled to take the first on the list.

He said that at Bandon a large factory had been closed through the efforts of the men to get higher wages, ditto at Belfast, and 'it was calculated that wages to the amount of £500,000 per year were lost to Dublin by trade unions. The combination of tailors in that city, for instance, had raised the price of clothes to such a pitch that it was worth a person's while to go to Glasgow and wait a couple of days for a suit, the difference in the price paying the expense of the trip.' He also ascribed the disapperance of the ship-building trade from Dublin to the evil effects of trade unions.

Because of O'Connell's speech his friends, the Whig government, appointed a committee, not to enquire into the Glasgow cases, but to investigate the acts of the Irish, and especially of the Dublin trade unions. The Special Committee sat and collected two volumes of evidence, O'Connell producing a number of witnesses to bear testimony against the Irish trade unionists, but the report of the committee was never presented to the House of Commons.

In June of the same year, 1838, O'Connell had another opportunity to vent his animus against the working class, and serve the interest of English and Irish capitalism, and was not slow to take advantage of it. In the year 1833, mainly owing to the efforts of the organised factory operatives, and some high-spirited philanthropists, a law had been enacted forbidding the employment of children *under nine years of age* in factories except silk mills, and forbidding those under thirteen from working more than forty-eight hours per week, or nine hours per day. The ages mentioned will convey to the reader some idea of how infantile flesh and blood had been sacrificed to sate the greed of the propertied class. Yet this eminently moderate enactment was fiercely hated by the godly capitalists of England, and by every unscrupulous device they could contrive they strove to circumvent it.

So constant and effective was their evasion of its merciful provisions that on 23 June the famous friend of the factory operatives, Lord Ashley, in the House of Commons, moved as an amendment to the Order of the Day the second reading of a 'Bill to more effectually regulate Factory Works', its purpose being to prevent or punish any further infringement of the Act of 1833. O'Connell opposed the motion, and attempted to justify the infringement of the law by the employers by stating that 'they (parliament) had legislated against the nature of things, and against the right of industry'.

'Let them not,' he said, 'be guilty of the childish folly of regulating the labour of adults, and go about parading before their world *their ridiculous humanity*, which would end by converting their manufacturers into beggars'. The phrase about regulating the labour of adults was borrowed from the defence set up by the capitalists that preventing the employment of children also interfered with the labour of adults — freeborn Englishmen! O'Connell was not above using this clap-trap, as he on the previous occasion had not been above making the lying pretence that the enforcement of a *minimum* wage prevented the payment of *high* wages to any specially skilled artisan.

On this question of the attitude to be taken towards the claims of labour, O'Connell differed radically with one of his most capable lieutenants, Fergus O'Connor. The latter being returned to parliament as a repealer was struck by the miserable condition of the real people of England in whose interests Ireland was supposed to be governed, and as a result of its investigation into its cause arrived at the conclusion that the basis of the oppression of Ireland was economic, that labour in England was oppressed by the same class and by the operation of the same causes as had impoverished and ruined Ireland, and that the solution of the problem in both countries required the union of the democracies in one common battle against their oppressors.

He earnestly strove to impress this view upon O'Connell, only to find that in the latter class feeling was much stronger than desire for Irish national freedom, and that he, O'Connell, felt himself to be much more akin to the propertied class of England than to the working class of Ireland. This was proved by his actions in the cases above cited.

This divergence of opinion between O'Connell and O'Connor closed Ireland to the latter and gave him to the Chartists as one of their most fearless and trusted leaders. When he died, more than 50,000 toilers marched in the funeral procession which bore his remains to his last resting-place. He was one of the first of that long list of Irish fighters in Great Britain whose unselfish sacrifices have gone to make a record for an 'English' labour movement.

That the propertied and oppressing classes were well aware of the value of O'Connell's services against the democracy, and were believed to be grateful for the same, was attested by the action of Richard Lalor Shiel when, defending him during the famous State trials, he claimed the consideration of the court for O'Connell because he had stood between the people of Ireland and the people of England, and so 'prevented a junction which would have formidable enough to overturn any administration that could be formed.'

But as zealous as O'Connell and the middle class repealers were to prevent any international action of the democracies, the Irish working class were as enthusiastic in their desire to consummate it. Irish Chartist Associations sprang up all over the island, and we are informed by a writer in the **United Irishman** of John Mitchel, 1848, that in Dublin they had grown so strong and so hostile to O'Connellism that at one time negotiations were in progress for a public debate between the Liberator and a representative of the Dublin trades. But upon the arrest and imprisonment of O'Connell, he continues, the working class were persuaded to abandon their separate organisations for the sake of presenting a common front to the government, a step they afterwards regretted.

To this letter, John Mitchel, as editor, appended a note reminding his readers of the anti-labour record of O'Connell, and adducing it as a further reason for repudiating his leadership. Yet it is curious that in his **History of Ireland**, Mitchel omits all reference to this disgraceful side of O'Connell's career, as do indeed all the other Irish 'Historians'. If silence gives consent, then all our history(?) writing scribes have consented to, and hence approved of, this suppression of the facts of history in order to assist in perpetuating the blindness and the subjection of labour.

Chapter Thirteen

OUR IRISH GIRONDINS SACRIFICE THE IRISH PEASANTRY UPON THE ALTAR OF PRIVATE PROPERTY

'There is a class of revolutionists called Girondists whose fate in history is remarkable enough. Men who rebel, and urge the lower classes to rebel, ought to have other than formulas to go upon. Men who discern in the misery of the toiling, complaining millions, not misery but only a raw material which can be wrought upon and traded in for one's own poor hide-bound theories and egoisms, to whom millions of living fellow-creatures with beating hearts in their bosoms — beating, suffering, hoping — are 'masses', mere explosive masses, for blowing down Bastilles with, for voting at hustings for "us", such men are of the questionable species.' — *Thomas Carlyle*

THE OUTBREAK of the famine, which commenced on a small scale in 1845, and increased its area and intensity until 1849, brought to a head the class antagonism in Ireland, of which the rupture with the trades was one manifestation, and again revealed the question of property as the test by which the conduct of public men is regulated, even when those men assume the garb of revolution.

Needless to say, this is not the interpretation of the history of that awful period we are given by the orthodox Irish or English writers upon that subject. Irish nationalists of all stripes and English critics of every variety agree with wonderful unanimity in ascribing a split in the Repeal Association which led to the formation by the seceders of the body known as the 'Irish Confederation' to the academic question of whether force might or might not be employed to achieve a political end.

The majority of the Repeal Association, we are told, subscribed to the principle enunciated by O'Connell that 'the greatest sublunary blessings were not worth the shedding of a single drop of human blood', and John Mitchel, Father Meehan, Gavan Duffy, Thomas Francis Meagher, Devin Reilly, William Smith O'Brien, Fintan Lalor, and others repudiated that doctrine, and on this point of purely theoretical divergence the secession from O'Connell took place.

It is difficult to believe that any large number of Irishmen ever held such a doctrine seriously; it is quite certain that the Irish Catholic priesthood, O'Connell's chief lieutenants, did not hold nor counsel such a doctrine during the Tithe War. O'Connell himself had declared that he would willingly join in helping England in 'bringing down the American Eagle in its highest pride of flight', which surely would have involved war, and in the House of Commons on one occasion, in reply to Lord Lyndhurst, who had characterised the Irish as 'aliens in blood, in language, and in religion', Richard Lalor Shiel, a champion of O'Connellism, had delivered a magnificent oration vaunting of the prowess of the Irish soldiers in the English army. In passing we note that Shiel considered the above phrase of Lord Lyndhurst an insult; modern Irish Nationalists triumphantly assert the idea embodied in that phrase as the real basis of Irish nationalism.

Nor yet were the seceders, the Young Irelanders as they were called, in favour of physical force, save as a subject for flights in poetry and oratory. In reality the secession took place on a false issue; the majority on either side being disciplined to admit, even if they recognised, the real issue dividing them. That issue was the old and ever present one of the democratic principle in human society versus the aristocratic.

The Young Irelanders, young and enthusiastic, felt the force of the democratic principle then agitating European society, indeed the very name of Young Ireland was an adaptation of the names used by the Italian revolutionist Mazzini for the revolutionary associations, Young Italy, Young Switzerland, Young France, and Young Germany, he founded after the year 1831. And as the progress of the revolutionary movement on the Continent, accompanied as it was by the popularisation of socialist ideas among the revolutionary masses, synchronised with the falling apart of the social system in Ireland following the famine, the leaders of the Young Ireland party responded to and moved along with the revolutionary current of events without ever being able to comprehend the depth and force of the stream upon whose surface they were embarked. The truth of this is apparent to all who study their action when at last the long talked of day for revolution had arrived.

By that time, 1848, Ireland was in the throes of the greatest famine in her history.

A few words explanatory of that famine may not be amiss to some of our readers. The staple food of the Irish peasantry was the potato; all other agricultural produce, grains and cattle, was sold to pay the landlord's rent. The ordinary value of the potato crop was yearly approximately twenty million pounds in English money; in 1848, in the midst of the famine, the value of agricultural produce in Ireland was £44,958,120.

In that year the entire potato crop was a failure and to that fact the famine is placidly attributed, yet those figures amply prove that there was food enough in the country to feed double the population were the laws of capitalist society set aside, and human rights elevated to their proper position. It is a common saying amongst Irish Nationalists that 'Providence sent the potato blight but England made the famine.' The statement is true, and only needs amending by adding that 'England made the famine by a rigid application of the economic principles that lie at the base of capitalist society.'

No man who accepts capitalist society and the laws thereof can logically find fault with the statesmen of England for their acts in that awful period. They stood for the rights of property and free competition, and philosophically accepted their consequences upon Ireland; the leaders of the Irish people also stood for the rights of property, and refused to abandon them even when they saw their consequences in the slaughter by famine of over a million of the toilers.

The first failure of the potato crop took place in 1845, and between September and December of that year 515 deaths from hunger were registered, although 3,250,000 quarters of wheat and numberless cattle had been exported. From that time until 1850 the famine spread, and the exports of food continued. Thus in 1848 it was estimated that 300,000 persons died of hunger and 1,826,132 quarters of wheat and barley were exported.

Typhus fever, which always follows on the heels of hunger, struck down as many as perished directly of famine, until at last it became impossible in many districts to get sufficient labourers with strength enough to dig separate graves for the dying. Recourse was had to famine pits, into which the bodies were thrown promiscuously; whole families died in their miserable cabins, and lay and rotted there, and travellers in remote parts of the country often stumbled upon villages in which the whole population had died of hunger.

In 1847, 'black '47', 250,000 died of fever, 21,770 of starvation. Owing to the effects of emigration agents and remittances sent from relatives abroad in the same year, 89,783 persons embarked for Canada. They were flying from hunger, but they could not fly from the fever that follows in the wake of hunger, and 6,100 died and were thrown overboard on the voyage, and 4,100 died on their arrival in Canada, 5,200 in hospitals, and 1,900 in interior towns.

Great Britain was nearer than America, and many who could not escape to the latter rushed to the inhospitable shores of the former; but pressure was brought to bear upon the steamship companies, and they raised the rates upon all passengers by steerage to an almost prohibitive price. In this flight to England occurred one of the most fearful tragedies of all history, a tragedy which, in our opinion, surpasses that of the Black Hole of Calcutta in its accumulation of fearful and gruesome horrors.

On 2 December 1848, a steamer left Sligo with 220 steerage passengers on board bound for Liverpool. On that bleak northwestern coast such a passage is at all times rough, and storms are both sudden and fierce. Such a storm came on during the night, and as the unusual number of passengers crowded the deck the crew unceremoniously and brutally drove them below decks and battened down the hatches to prevent their re-emergence. In the best of weather the steerage of such a coasting vessel is, even when empty of human freight, foul, suffocating and unbearable; the imagination fails to realise what it must have been on that awful night when 200 poor wretches were driven into its depths.

To add to the horror, when some of the more desperate beat upon the hatches and demanded release, the mate, in a paroxysm of rage, ordered tarpaulin to be thrown across the opening to stifle their cries. It did stifle their cries, it also exluded the air and the light, and there in that inferno those 200 human beings fought, struggled and gasped for air while the elements warred outside and the frail tub of a ship was tossed upon the surface of the waters.

At last, when some one stronger than the rest managed to break through and reached the deck, he confronted the ship's officers with the grim news that their brutality had made them murderers, that grim death was reaping his harvest amongst the passengers. It was too true. Out of the 200 passengers battened below decks, 72, more than a third of the entire number, had expired, suffocated for want of air or mangled to death in the blind struggle of despair in the darkness. Such is the tale of that voyage of the ship *Londonderry*, surely the most horrible tale of the sea in the annals of any white people!

Amidst such conditions the Irish Confederation had been preaching the moral righteousness of rebellion, and discoursing learnedly in English to a starving people, the most of whom knew only Irish, about the historical examples of Holland, Belgium, Poland, and the Tyrol.

A few men, notably John Mitchel, James Fintan Lalor, and Thomas Devin Reilly, to their credit, be it said, openly advocated, as the first duty of the people, their refusal to pay rents, the retention of their crops to feed their own families, and the breaking up of bridges and tearing up of railroad lines in order to prevent the removal of food from the country. Had such advice been followed by the Young Irelanders as a body it would, as the events showed, have been enthusiastically adopted by the people at large, in which event no force in the power of England could have saved landlordism or the British Empire in Ireland.

As explained by Fintan Lalor, the keenest intellect in Ireland in his day, it meant the avoidance of all pitched battles with the English army, and drawing it into a struggle along lines and on a plan of campaign where its discipline, training and methods would be a hindrance rather than a help, and where no mobilisation, battalion drilling, nor technical knowledge of military science was required of the insurgent masses.

In short, it involved a social and a national revolution, each resting upon the other.

But the men who advocated this were in a hopeless minority, and the chiefs of the Young Irelanders were as rabidly solicitous about the rights of the landlord as were the chiefs of the English government. While the people perished the Young Irelanders talked, and their talk was very beautiful, thoroughly grammatical, nicely polished, and the proper amounts of passion introduced always at the proper psychological moment. But still the people perished.

Eventually the government seized upon the really dangerous man — the man who had hatred of injustice deeply enough rooted to wish to destroy it at all costs, the man who had faith enough in the masses to trust a revolutionary outbreak to their native impulses, and who possessed the faculty of combining thought with action, John Mitchel.

With his arrest the people looked for immediate revolution, so did the government, so did Mitchel himself. All were disappointed. John Mitchel was carried off to penal servitude in Van Dieman's Land (Tasmania) after scornfully refusing to sign a manifesto presented to him in his cell by Thomas Meagher and others, counselling the people *not* to attempt to rescue him.

The working class of Dublin and most of the towns were clamouring for their leaders to give the words for a rising; in many places in the country the peasants were acting spontaneously. Eventually news reaching Dublin in July 1848 that warrants were issued for the arrest of the chiefs of the Young Ireland party, they determined to appeal to the country. But everything had to be done in a 'respectable' manner; English army on one side, provided with guns, bands and banners; Irish army on the other side, also provided with guns, bands and banners, 'serried ranks with glittering steel', no mere proletarian insurrection, and no interference with the rights of property.

When C G Duffy was arrested on Saturday 9 July, in Dublin,

the Dublin workers surrounded the military escort on the way to the prison at Newgate, stopped the carriage, pressed up to Duffy and offered to begin the insurrection then and there. 'Do you wish to be rescued?' said one of the leaders, 'Certainly not,' said Duffy. And the puzzled toilers fell back and allowed the future Australian premier to go to prison. In Cashel, Tipperary, Michael Doheny was arrested. The people stormed the jail and rescued him. He insisted upon giving himself up again and applied for bail.

In Waterford Meagher was arrested. As he was being taken through the city guarded by troops the people erected a barricade in the way across a narrow bridge over the River Suir, and when the carriage reached the bridge some cut the trace of the horses and brought the cavalcade to a standstill. Meagher ordered them to remove the barricade; they begged him to give the word for insurrection and they would begin then and there. The important city was in their hands, but Meagher persisted in going with the soldiers, and the poor working class rebels of Waterford let him go crying out as they did so, 'You will regret it, you will regret it, and it is your own fault.' Meagher afterwards proved himself a fearless soldier of a regular army, but as an insurgent he lacked the necessary initiative.

But the crowning absurdity of all was the leadership of William Smith O'Brien. He wandered through the country telling the starving peasantry to get ready, but refusing to allow them to feed themselves at the expense of the landlords who had so long plundered, starved, and evicted them; he would not allow his followers to seize upon the carts of grain passing along the roads where the people were dying for want of food; at Mullinahone he refused to allow his followers to fell trees to build a barricade across the road until they had asked permission of the landlords who owned the trees; when the people of Killenaule had a body of dragoons entrapped between two barricades he released the dragoons from their dangerous situation upon their leader assuring him that he had no warrant for his, O'Brien's, arrest; in another place he surprised a party of soldiers in the Town Hall with their arms taken apart for cleaning purposes, and instead of confiscating their arms he told the soldiers that their arms were as safe as they would be in Dublin Castle.

When we remember the state of Ireland then, with her population perishing of famine, all the above recital reads like a page of comic opera. Unfortunately it is not; it is a page from the blackest period of Ireland's history. Reading it we can understand why Smith O'Brien has a monument in Dublin, although Fintan Lalor's name and writings were boycotted for more than fifty years.

W A O'Connor, BA, in his **History of the Irish People**, sums up Smith O'Brien's career thus: 'The man had broken up a peaceful oganisation in the cause of war, promised war to a people in desperate strait, went into a country to wage war, then considered it guilt to do any act of war.' It must, of course, be conceded that Smith O'Brien was a man of high moral probity, but it is equally necessary to affirm that he was a landlord vehemently solicitous for the rights of his class, and allowing his solicitude for those rights to stand between the millions of the Irish race and their hopes of life and freedom. It ought, however, also to be remembered, in extenuation of his conduct in that awful crisis, the he had inherited vast estates as the result of the social, national, and religious apostasy of his forefathers, and in view of such an ancestry it is more wonderful that he had dreamed of rebellion than that he had repudiated revolution.

Had socialist principles been applied to Ireland in those days not one person need have died of hunger, and not one cent of charity need have been subscribed to leave a smirch upon the Irish name. But all except a few men had elevated landlord property and capitalist political economy to a fetish to be worshipped, and upon the altar of that fetish Ireland perished. At the lowest computation 1,225,000 persons died of absolute hunger; all of these were sacrificed upon the altar of capitalist thought.

Early in the course of the famine the English premier, Lord John Russell, declared that nothing must be done to interfere with private enterprise on the regular course of trade, and this was the settled policy of the government from first to last. A Treasury 'Minute' of 31 August 1846, provided that 'depôts for the sale of food were to be established at Longford, Banagher, Limerick, Galway, Waterford, and Sligo, and subordinate depôts at other places on the western coast', but the rules provided that such depôts were not to be opened where food could be obtained from private dealers, and when opened food was to be sold at prices which would permit of private dealers competing.

In all the Acts establishing relief works it was stipulated that all the labour must be entirely unproductive, so as not to prevent capitalists making a profit either then or in the future. Private dealers made fortunes ranging from £40,000 to £80,000.

In 1845 a Commissariat Relief Department was organised to bring in Indian corn for sale in Ireland, but *none was to be sold until all private stores were sold out*. The State of Massachusetts hired an American ship-of-war, the *Jamestown*, loaded it with grain and sent it to Ireland; the government placed the cargo in storage, claiming that putting it on the market would disturb trade.

A Poor Relief Bill in 1847 made provision for the employment of labour on public works, but stipulated that none should be employed who retained more than a quarter of an acre of land; this induced tens of thousands to surrender their farms for the sake of a bit to eat and saved the landlords all the trouble and expense of eviction. When this had been accomplished to a sufficient extent 734,000 persons were discharged, and as they had given up their farms to get employment on the works they were now as helpless as men on a raft in mid ocean. Mr Mulhall, in his **Fifty Years of National Progress** estimates the number of persons evicted between 1838 and 1888 as 3,668,000; the greater number of these saw their homes destroyed during the years under consideration, and this Poor Relief Bill, nick-named an 'Eviction-Made-Easy Act', was one main weapon for their undoing.

In 1846, England, hitherto a Protectionist country, adopted Free Trade, ostensibly in order to permit corn to come freely and cheaply to the starving Irish. In reality, as Ireland was a corn and grain exporting country, the measure brought Continental agricultural produce to England into competition with that of Ireland, and hence by lowering agricultural prices still further intensified the misery of the Irish producing classes. The real meaning of the measure was that England, being a manufacturing nation, desired to cheapen food in order that its wage slaves might remain content with low wages, and indeed one of the most immediate results of free trade in England was a wholesale reduction of the wages of the manufacturing proletariat.

The English capitalist class, with that hypocrisy that everywhere characterises the class in its public acts, used the misery of the Irish as a means to conquer the opposition of the English landlord class to free trade in grains, but in this, as in every other measure of the famine years, they acted consistently upon the lines of capitalist political economy. Within the limits of that social system and its theories their acts are unassailable and unimpeachable; it is only when we reject that system and the intellectual and social fetters it imposes that we really acquire the right to denounce the English administration of Ireland during the famine as a colossal crime against the human race.

The non-socialist Irish man or woman who fumes against that administration is in the illogical position of denouncing an effect of whose cause he is a supporter. That cause was the system of capitalist property. With the exception of those few men we have before named, the Young Ireland leaders of 1848 failed to rise to the grandeur of the opportunity offered them to choose between human rights and property rights as a basis of nationality, and the measure of their failure was the measure of their country's disaster.

Chapter Fourteen

SOCIALISTIC TEACHING OF THE YOUNG IRELANDERS: THE THINKERS AND THE WORKERS

'What do ye at our door,
Ye guard our master's granaries from the thin hands of the poor.'

— *Lady Wilde* (Speranza)

'God of Justice, I cried, send thy spirit down
On those lords so cruel and so proud.
Soften their hearts and relax their frown,
Or else, I cried aloud,
Vouchsafe strength to the peasant's hand
To drive them at length from out of the land.'

— *Thomas Davis*

WE HAVE pointed out that the Young Ireland chiefs who had so fervently declaimed about the revolution were utterly incapable of accepting it when at last it presented itself to them, indeed Doheny used that very word in describing the scenes at Cashel. 'It was the revolution,' he said, 'if we had accepted it.' We might with perfect justice apply to these brilliant but unfortunate men the words of an other writer, Lissagaray, in describing a similar class of leaders in France, and say 'having all their life sung the glories of the Revolution, when it rose up before them they ran away appalled, like the arab fisher at the apparition of the genie'.

To the average historian who treats of the relations between Ireland and England as of a struggle between two nations, without any understanding of the economic conditions, or of the great world movements which caught both countries in their grasp, the hesitancy and vacillation of the Young Ireland chiefs in the crisis of their country's fate constitutes an insoluble problem and has too often been used to point a sneer at Irishmen when the writer was English, or to justify a sickening apology when the writer was Irish. Neither action is at all warranted.

The simple fact is that the Irish workers in town and country were ready and willing to revolt, and that the English government of the time was saved from serious danger only by the fact that Smith O'Brien and those who patterned after him dreaded to trust the nation to the passion of the so-called lower classes.

Had rebellion broken out at the time in Ireland the English Chartists who had been arming and preparing for a similar purpose would, as indeed Mitchel pointed out continually in his paper, have seized the occasion to take the field also. Many regiments of the English army were also honeycombed with revolt, and had repeatedly shown their spirit by publicly cheering for the Irish and Chartist cause. An English leader of the Chartists, John Frost, was sentenced to a heavy term of transportation for his seditious utterances at this time, and another great English champion of the working class, Ernest Jones, in commenting upon the case, declared defiantly in a public meeting that 'the time would come when John Mitchel and John Frost would be brought back, and Lord John Russell sent to take their place, and the Green Flag would fly in triumph over Downing Street and Dublin Castle,' Downing Street being the residence of the prime minister. For uttering this sentiment, Ernest Jones was arrested and sentenced to twelve months' imprisonment.

In their attitude towards all manifestation of working class revolt in England, the Young Irelanders were sorely divided. In his paper, **The United Irishman**, John Mitchel hailed it exultantly as an aid to Ireland, and as a presage of the victory of real democracy, setting aside a large portion of his space in every issue to chronicle the progress of the cause of the people in England. His attitude in this matter was one of the most potent causes of his enduring popularity amongst the masses.

On the other hand the section of Young Irelanders who had made Smith O'Brien their idol for no other discoverable reason than the fact that he was rich and most respectable, strove by every means in their power to dissociate the cause of Ireland from the cause of democracy.

A wordy war between Mitchel and his critics ensued, each side appealing to the precedent of 1798, with the result that Mitchel was easily able to prove that the revolutionists of that period — notably Wolfe Tone — had not allied the cause of Ireland with the cause of democracy in general, but had vehemently insisted upon the necessity of a social revolution in Ireland at the expense of the landed aristocracy. Copying from Fintan Lalor, Mitchel made the principles involved in those ideas the slogans of his revolutionary campaign. He correctly insisted upon a social insurrection, that the same insurrectionary upheaval that destroyed and ended the social subjection of the producing classes would end the hateful foreign tyranny reared upon it.

Two passages from his writings are especially useful as bearing out and attesting to his position on those points — points that are still the fiercest subjects of dispute in Ireland. In his 'Letter to the small farmers of Ireland', 4 March 1848, he says: 'But I am told it is vain to speak thus to you; that the peace policy of O'Connell is dearer to you than life and honour — that many of your clergy, too, exhort you to die rather than violate what the English call "law" — and that you are resolved to take their bidding. Then die — die in your patience and perseverance, but be well assured of this — that the priest who bids you perish patiently amidst your own golden harvest preaches the gospel of England, insults manhood and common sense, bears false witness against religion, and blasphemes the providence of God.'

When the Republican government which came into power in Paris after the revolution of February 1848, recognising that it owed its existence to the armed working men, and that those workers were demanding some security for their own class as a recompense for their bloody toil, enacted a law guaranteeing 'the right to work' to all, and pledging the credit of the nation to secure that right, Mitchel joyfully hailed that law as an indication that the absurd theories of what he rightfully styled the 'English system', or capitalism, had no longer a hold upon the minds of the French people. We quote a portion of that article. Our readers will note that Free Trade referred to is free trade in labour as against state protection of the rights of the worker:

> Dynasties and thrones are not half so important as workshops, farms and factories. Rather we may say that dynasties and thrones, and even provisional governments, are good for anything exactly in proportion as they secure fair play, justice and freedom to those who labour.
>
> It is here that France is really ahead of all the world. The great Third Revolution has overthrown the enlightened pedantic political economy (what we know in Ireland as the English political economy, or the Famine Political Economy), and has established once and for all the true and old principles of protection to labour, and the right and duty of combination among workmen.
>
> By a decree of the Provisional Government dated 25 February:
>
> It engages to guarantee work to all citizens. It recognises the right of workmen to combine for the purpose of enjoying the lawful proceeds of their labour.
>
> The French Republicans do not, like ignorant and barbarous English Whigs, recognise a right to pauper relief and make it a premium upon idleness. They know that man has a charter to eat bread in the sweat of his brow and not otherwise, and they acknowledge that highest and most sacred mission of government — to take care that bread may be had for the earning. For this reason, they expressly, and in set terms, renounce 'competition' and 'free trade' *in the sense in which an English Whig uses these words*, and deliberately adopt combination and protection — that the nation should combine to pretect by laws its own national industry, and that individuals should combine with other individuals to protect by trade associations the several branches of national industry.
>
> The free trade and competition — in other words the English system — is pretty well understood now; its obvious purpose and effect are to make the rich richer and the poor poorer, to make capital the absolute ruler of the world, and labour a blind

and helpless slave. By free trade the manufacturers of Manchester are enabled to clothe India, China, and South America, and the artisans of Manchester can hardly keep themselves covered from the cold. By dint of free trade Belfast grows more linen cloth than it ever did before; but the men who weave it have hardly a shirt to their backs. Free trade fills with corn the stores of speculating capitalists, but leaves those who have sown and reaped the corn without a meal. Free trade unpeoples villages and peoples poorhouses, consolidates farms and gluts the graveyards with famished corpses.

There is to be no more of this free trade in France. Men can no longer 'do what they like with their own' there.

February 1848 came, and the pretext of the reform banquet. Again Paris had her three days' agony, and was delivered of her third and fairest born revolution.

There could be no mistake this time; the rubbish of thrones and dynasties is swept out for ever, and the people sit sovereign in the land. One of their first and greatest acts is the enactment of a commission to inquire into the whole of the great labour question, and to all the documents issued by this commission appear signed the names of Louis Blanc and the insurgent Lyons, Albert Ouvrier (workman). He is not ashamed of his title, though now a great officer of the state. He is a working man, and is proud of it 'in any bond, bill, quittance, or obligation', *Ouvrier*.

Sixty-six years ago the farmers of France had their revolution. Eighteen years ago the 'respectable' middle class had theirs, and have made a good penny in it since, but upon this third and last all the world may see the stamp and impress of the man who made — Albert Ouvrier, his mark. We have all three revolutions to accomplish, and the sooner we set about it the better. Only let us hope all the work may be done in one. Let not the lessons of history be useless.

The detestable system of 'free trade' and 'fair competition' which is described by Louis Blanc as that 'specious system of leaving unrestricted all pecuniary dealing between man and man, which leaves the poor man at the mercy of the rich, and promises to cupidity that waits its time an easy victory over hunger that cannot wait'. The system that seeks to make Mammon and not God or justice rule this world — in one word the English or famine system — must be abolished utterly, in farms or workhops, in town and country, abolished utterly; and to do this were worth three revolutions, or three times three.

So wrote Mitchel when, burning with a holy hatred of tyranny, he poured the vitriol of his scorn upon all the pedants who strutted around him, pedants who were as scrupulous in polishing a phrase for a lecture as a sword for a parade — and incapable of advancing beyond either.

His joy was, as we know now, somewhat premature, as the government which passed the law was itself a capitalistic government, and as soon as it found itself strong enough, and had won over the army, repealed its own laws, and suppressed, with the most frightful bloodshed, the June insurrection of the workmen striving to enforce its fulfilment.

It is the latter insurrection which Mitchel denounces in his Jail Journal when, led astray by the garbled reports of English newspapers, he anathematises the very men whom he had in this article, when fuller sources of information were available, courageously and justly praised. But another revolutionist, Devin Reilly, in the **Irish Felon**, more correctly appraised the position of the June insurgents, and also appreciated the fact that Ireland for its redemption required something more far-reaching, something sounding deeper springs of human action, something more akin to the teachings that inspired the heroic workers of France than was to be found in the 'personal probity', or 'high principles', or 'aristocratic descent', or 'eminent respectability' of a few leaders.

When Mitchel was arrested and his paper suppressed, two other papers sprang up to take the post of danger thus left vacant. One, **The Irish Tribune**, represented the element which stood for the 'moral right of insurrection', and the other, the **Irish Felon**, embodied the ideas of those who insisted that the English conquest of Ireland was twofold, social, or economic, and political, and that therefore the revolution must also have these two aspects. These latter were at all times in the fullest sympathy with the movements of the working class democracy at home and abroad. John Martin edited the **Irish Felon**, James Fintan Lalor and Devin Reilly were its chief writers.

Reilly, who hailed originally from Monaghan, had long been a close observer and sympathiser with the movements of the working class, and all schemes of social redemption. As a writer on the **Nation** newspaper he had contributed a series of articles on the great French socialist, Louis Blanc, in a review of his great work **Dix Ans** (Ten Years), in which, while dissenting from the 'state socialistic' schemes of social regeneration favoured by Blanc he yet showed the keenest appreciation of the gravity and universality of the social question, as well as grasping the innate heroism and sublimity of the working class movement.

This attitude he preserved to the last of his days. When in exile in America, after the insurrection, he was chosen by the printers of Boston to edit a paper, the **Protective Union**, they had founded on co-operative principles to advocate the rights of labour, and was thus one of the first pioneers of labour journalism in the United States — a proud and fitting position for a true Irish revolutionist. As writer in the **American Review**, he wrote a series of articles on the European situation, of which Horace Greeley said that if collected and published as a book they would create a revolution in Europe.

Commenting upon the uprising in France in June he says in the **Irish Felon**:

> We are not Communists — we abhor communism for the same reason we abhor poor law systems, and systems founded on the absolute sovereignty of wealth. Communism destroys the independence and dignity of labour, makes the workingman a state pauper and takes his manhood from him. But, communism or no communism, these 70,000 workmen had a clear right to existence — they had the best right to existence of any men in France, and if they could have asserted their right by force of arms they would have been fully justified. *The social system in which a man willing to work is compelled to starve is a blasphemy, an anarchy, and no system.*

> For the present these victims of monarchic rule, disowned by the republic, are conquered; 10,000 are slain, 20,000 perhaps doomed to the Marquesas. *But for all that the rights of labour are not conquered, and will not and cannot be conquered. Again and again the labourer will rise up against the idler — the workingman will meet this bourgeoisie, and grapple and war with them till their equality is established, not in word, but in fact.*

This was the spirit of the men grouped around the **Irish Felon**, its editor alone excepted. Students of socialism will recognise that many who are earnest workers for socialism today would, like Devin Reilly, have 'abhorred' the crude Communism of 1848. The fact that he insisted upon the unqualified right of the working class to work out its own salvation, by force of arms if necessary, is what entitled Devin Reilly to a high place of honour in the estimation of the militant proletariat of Ireland.

The opening passage in an 'Address of the Medical Students of Dublin to All Irish Students of Science and Art', adopted at a meeting held in Northumberland Building, Eden Quay, on 4 April 1848, and signed by John Savage as chairman and Richard Dalton Williams as secretary, shows also that amongst the educated young men of that generation there was a general recognition of the fact that the struggle of Ireland against her oppressors was naturally linked with and ought to be taken in conjunction with the world-wide movement of the democracy. It says 'a war is waging at this hour all over Europe between Intelligence and Labour on the one side and Despotism and Force on the other', a sentiment which Joseph Brennan versified in a poem on 'Divine Right', in which the excellence of the sentiment must be held to atone for the poverty of the poetry. One verse says:

The only right acknowledged
By the people living now,
Is the right to obtain honour
By the sweat of brain and brow.
The Right Divine of Labour
To be first of earthly things,
That the Thinker and the Worker
Are manhood's only kings.

But the palm of honour for the clearest exposition of the doctrine of revolution, social and political, must be given to James Fintan Lalor, of Tenakill, Queen's County. Lalor, unfortunately, suffered from a slight physical disability, which incapacitated him from attaining to any leadership other than intellectual, a fact that in such a time and amidst such apeople was fatal to his immediate influence. Yet in his writings, as we study them today, we find principles of action and of society which have within them not only the best plan of campaign suited for the needs of a country seeking its freedom through insurrection against a dominant nation, but also held the seeds of the more perfect social peace of the future.

All his writings at this period are so illuminating that we find it difficult to select from the mass any particular passages which more deserve reproduction than others. But as an indication of the line of argument pursued by this peerless thinker and as a welcome contrast to the paralysing respect, nay, reverence, for landlordism shown by Smith O'Brien and his worshippers, perhaps the following passages will serve.

In an article entitled 'The Faith of a Felon', published 8 July 1848, he tells how he had striven to convert the Irish Confederation to his views and failed, and says:

> They wanted an alliance with the landowners. They chose to consider them as Irishmen, and imagined they could induce them to hoist the green flag. They wished to preserve an aristocracy. They desired, not a democratic, but merely a national revolution. Had the Confederation in the May or June of '47 thrown heart and mind and means into the movement I pointed out they would have made it successful, and settled at once and forever all questions between us and England. The opinions I then stated, and which I yet stand firm to, are these:
>
> 1. That in order to save their own lives, the occupying tenants of the soil of Ireland ought, next autumn, to refuse all rent and arrears of rent then due, beyond and except the value of the overplus of harvest produce remaining in their lands after having deducted and reserved a due and full provision for their own subsistence during the next ensuing twelve months.

> 2. That they ought to refuse and resist being made beggars, landless and homeless, under the English law of ejection.
> 3. That they ought further, *on principle*, to refuse *all rent* to the present usurping proprietors, until the people, the *true proprietors* (or lords paramount, in legal parlance) have, in national congress or convention, decided what rents they are to pay, and to whom they are to pay them.
> 4. And that the people, on grounds of policy and economy, ought to decide (as a general rule admitting or reservations) that these rents shall be paid to *themselves*, the people, for public purposes, and for behoof and benefit of them, the entire general people.
> It has been said to me that such a war, on the principles I propose, would be looked on with detestation by Europe. I assert the contrary; I say such a war would propagate itself throughout Europe. Mark the words of this prophecy — the principle I propound goes to the foundations of Europe, and sooner or later will cause Europe to outrise. *Mankind will yet be masters of the earth*. The right of the people to make the laws — this produced the first great modern earthquake, whose latent shocks, even now, are heaving in the heart of the world. The right of the people to own the land — this will produce the next. Train your hands, and your sons' hands, gentlemen of the earth, for you and they will yet have to use them.

The paragraph is significant as demonstrating that Fintan Lalor, like all the really dangerous revolutionists in Ireland, advocated his principles as part of the creed of the democracy of the world, and not merely as applicable only to the incidents of the struggle in Ireland against England. But this latter is the interpretation which the middle class politicians and historians of Ireland have endeavoured to give his teachings after the failure of their attempt, continued for half a century, to ignore or suppress all reference to his contribution to Irish revolutionary literature.

The working class democracy of Ireland will, it is to be hoped, be, for their part, as assertive of the universality of Lalor's sympathies as their bourgeois compatriots are in denying it. That working class would be uselessly acquiescing in the smirching of its own record were it to permit emasculation of the message of this Irish apostle of revolutionary socialism.

And in emphasising this catholicity of his sympathies as well as the keenness of his insight into the social structure, that Irish working class will do well to confront the apostate patriotism of the politicians and anti-socialists of Ireland with the following brilliant passage from the work already quoted, and thus show how Lalor answered the plea of those who begged him to moderate or modify his position, to preach it as a necessity of Ireland's then desperate condition, and not as a universal principle.

> I attest and urge the plea of utter and desperate necessity to fortify her (Ireland's) claim, but, not to found it. *I rest it on no temporary and passing conditions, but on principles that are permanent, and imperishable, and universal — available to all times and to all countries as well as to our own* — I pierce through the upper stratum of occasional and shifting circumstances to bottom and base on the rock below. I put the question in its eternal form — the form in which, how often so ever suppressed for a season it can never be finally subdued, but will remain and return, outliving and outlasting the cowardice and corruption of generations. I view it as ages will view it — *not through the mists of a famine, but by the living lights of the firmament.*

By such lights the teachings of Fintan Lalor are being viewed today, with the result that, as he recedes from us in time his grandeur as a thinker is more and more recognised; his form rises clearer and more distinct to our view as the forms of the petty agitators and phrasemongering rebels who seemed to dominate the scene at that historic period sink into their proper place as unconscious factors in the British imperial plan of conquest by famine.

Cursed by the fatal gift of eloquence, our Irish Girondins of the Confederation enthralled the Irish people and intoxicated themselves out of the possibility of serious thinking; drunken with words they failed to realise that the ideas originating with Fintan Lalor and in part adopted and expounded with such dramatic power by Mitchel, were a more serious menace to the hated power of England than any the dream of a union of classes could ever materialise on Irish soil; the bones of the famine victims whitening on every Irish hill and valley or tossing on every wave of the Atlantic was the price Ireland paid for the eloquence of its rebels, and their scornful rejection of the socialistic teachings of its thinkers.

Chapter Fifteen

SOME MORE IRISH PIONEERS OF THE SOCIALIST MOVEMENT

'Either the Sermon on the Mount can rule this world or it cannot. The devil has a right to rule if we let him, but he has no right to call his rule Christian Civilisation.' —*John Boyle O'Reilly*

LOOKING BACKWARD to that eventful period (after 1848) we can now see that all hopes of a revolutionary movement had perished for that generation, had been strangled in the love embraces of our Girondins; but that fact naturally was not so apparent to the men of the time.

Hence it is not to be wondered at that journalistic activity on the part of the revolutionists did not cease with the suppression of the **United Irishman**, the **Irish Tribune**, or the **Irish Felon**. A small fugitive publication entitled the **Irish National Guard**, published apparently by a body of courageous Dublin workingmen of advanced opinions, also led a chequered existence championing the cause of revolution, and in January 1849 another paper, **The Irishman**, was set on foot by Bernard Fullam, who had been business manager of the **Nation**.

Fullam also started a new organisation, the 'Democratic Association', which is described as 'an association with aims almost entirely socialistic and revolutionary'. This association also spread amongst the Irish workers in Great Britain, and had the cordial support and endorsement of Feargus O'Connor, who saw in it the realisation of his long-hoped for dream of a common programme uniting the democracies of Ireland and Great Britain.

But the era of revolution was past for that generation in both countries, and it was too late for the working class revolutionists to repair the harm the middle class doctrines had done. The paper died in May 1850, after an existence of seventeen months. Among its contributors was Thomas Clarke Luby, afterwards one of the chief writers on the staff of the **Irish People**, organ of the Fenian Brotherhood, a fact that explains much of the advanced doctrine advocated by that journal. Another of the staff of the **Irishman** in those days was Joseph Brennan, whom we have already quoted as writing in the **Irish Tribune**. Brennan finally emigrated to America and contributed largely to the pages of the New Orleans **Delta**, many of poems in that journal showing the effects of his early association with the currents of social-revolutionary thought in Ireland.

Before leaving this period a few words should be said of the impress left upon the labour movement of Great Britain by the working class Irish exiles. An English writer, H S Foxwell, has said that 'Socialist propagandism has been mainly carried on by men of Celtic or Semitic blood,' and however true that may be, as a general statement, it is at least certain that to the men of Celtic blood the English-speaking countries are indebted for the greater part of the early propaganda of the socialist conception of society.

We have already referred to Feargus O'Connor; another Irishman who carved his name deep on the early structures of the labour and socialist movement in England as an author and Chartist leader was James Bronterre O'Brien. Among his best known works are: 'Rise, Progress and Phases of Human Slavery: How it came into the world, and how it may be made to go out of it', published in 1830; 'Address to the Oppressed and Mystified people of Great Britain', 1851; 'European Letters'; and the pages of the 'National Reformer', which he founded in 1837. At first an advocate of physical force, he in his later days gave himself up almost exclusively to the development of a system of land banks, in which he believed he had found a way to circumvent the political and military power of the capitalist class. Bronterre O'Brien is stated to have been the first to coin in England the distinctive title of 'social democrat', as an appellation for the adherents of the new order.

An earlier Irish apostle of the socialist movement of the working class, John Doherty, is much less known to the present generation than O'Brien, yet his methods bore more of the marks of constructive revolutionary statesmanship, and his message was equally clear. He appears to have been an almost dominant figure in the labour movement of England and Ireland between the year 1830 and 1840, spent little time in the development of socialist theories, but devoted all his energies to organising the working class and teaching it to act on its own initiative. He was general secretary of the 'Federation of Spinning Societies', which aimed to unite all the textile industries in one great national industrial union and was widespread through Great Britain and Ireland; he founded a 'National Association for the Protection of Labour', which directed its efforts towards building up a union of the working class effective alike for economic and political ends, and reached to 100,000 members, the Belfast trades applying in a body for affiliation; he founded and edited a paper, **The Voice of the People**, in 1831, which, although sevenpence per copy, attained to a circulation of 30,000, and is described as 'giving great attention to Radical politics, and the progress of evolution on the Continent'.

In his **History of Trades Unionism**, Sidney Webb quotes Francis Place — the best informed man in the labour movement in the England of his day — as declaring that during the English Reform Bill crisis in 1832 Doherty, instead of being led astray, as many labour leaders were, to rally to the side of the middle class reformers, was 'advising the working class to use the occasion for a social revolution.' This was indeed the keynote of Doherty's message; whatever was to be done was to be done by the working class. He is summed up as of 'wide information, great natural shrewdness, and far-reaching aims.' Was born in Larne in 1799.

Another Doherty, Hugh, attained to some prominence in socialistic circles in England, and we find him in 1841 in London editing a socialist paper, **The Phalanx**, which devoted itself to the propagation of the views of the French socialist, Fourier. It had little influence on the labour movement owing to its extremely doctrinaire attitude, but appears to have had circulation and correspondents in the United States. It was one of the first journals to be set up by a type-setting machine, and one of its numbers contains a minute description of the machine, which forms curious reading today.

In general the effect upon the English labour movement of the great influx of Irish workers seems to us to have been beneficial. It is true that their competition for employment had at first a seriously evil effect upon wages, but, on the other hand, a study of the fugitive literature of the movement of that time shows that the working class Irish exiles were present and active in the ranks of militant labour in numbers out of all proportion to the ratio they bore to the population at large. And always they were the advanced, the least compromising, the most irreconcilable element in the movement.

Of course the socialist sectarians and philosophers did not love the Irish — Charles Kingsley, that curious combination of prelate, socialist, chauvinist and virulent bigot, can scarcely remain within the bounds of decent language when he brings an Irishman into the thread of his narratives — but the aversion was born out of their fears of the Irish workers' impatience of compromise and eagerness for action. And hence the very qualities which endeared the Irish worker to the earnest rebel against capitalist iniquity estranged him from the affection of those whose social position enabled them to become the historians of his movements.

Chapter Sixteen

THE WORKING CLASS: THE INHERITORS OF THE IRISH IDEALS OF THE PAST — THE REPOSITORY OF THE HOPES OF THE FUTURE

'Is a Christian to starve, to submit, to bow down
As at some high consecrated behest,
Hugging close the old maxims, that "Weakness is strength",
And "Whatsoever is the best"?
O, texts of debasement! O, creed of deep shame!
O, Gospel of infamy treble,
Who strikes when he's struck, and takes when he starves,
In the eyes of the Lord is no rebel.'

J F O'Donnell

THIS BOOK does not aspire to be a history of labour in Ireland; it is rather a record of labour in Irish history. For that reason the plan of the book has precluded any attempt to deal in detail with the growth, development, or decay of industry in Ireland, except as it affected our general argument. That argument called for an explanation of the position of labour in the great epochs of our modern history, and with the attitude of Irish leaders towards the hopes, aspirations, and necessities of those who live by labour.

Occasionally, as when analysing the 'prosperity' of Grattan's Parliament, and the decay of Irish trade following the Legislative Union of 1800, we have been constrained to examine the fundamental causes which make for the progress, industrially or commercially, of some nations and the retrogression of others. For this apparent digression no apology is made, and none is called for; it was impossible to present our readers with a clear idea of the historical position of labour at any given moment without explaining the economic and political causes which contributed to make possible or necessary its attitude.

For the same reason it has been necessary sometimes to retrace our footsteps over some period already covered in order to draw attention to a phase of the subject, the introduction of which in the previous narrative would have marred the view of the question then under examination. Thus the origin of trade unionism in Ireland has not been dealt with, although in the course of our study we have shown that the Irish trades were well organised. Nor are we now prepared to enter upon that subject. Perhaps at some more propitious movement we will be enabled to examine the materials bearing upon the matter, and trace the growth of the institution in Ireland.

Sufficient for the present to state that Trades Guilds existed in Ireland as upon the Continent and England, during Roman Catholic, pre-Reformation days; that after the Reformation those Trade Guilds became exclusively Protestant, and even anti-Catholic, within the English Pale; that they continued to refuse admission to Catholics even after the passage of the Catholic Emancipation Act, and that these old Trades Guilds were formally abolished by law in 1840. But the Catholic and Protestant workmen who were excluded from guild membership (Episcopalians only being eligible) did nevertheless organise themselves, and it was their trade unions which dominated the labour world to the wrath of the capitalists and landlords, and the chagrin of the governments.

One remarkable and instructive feature of their organisation in town and country was the circumstance that every attempt at political rebellion in Ireland was always preceded by a remarkable development of unrest, discontent, and class consciousness amongst their members, demonstrating clearly that to the mind of the thoughtful Irish worker political and social subjection was very nearly related.

In the **Dublin Chronicle**, 28 January 1792, there is a record of a great strike of the journeymen tailors of Dublin, in the course of which, it is stated, armed tailors went to the workrooms of Messrs Miller, Ross Lane, Leet, Merchant's Quay, Walsh, Castle Street, and Ward, Cope Street, attacked certain scabs who were working there, cut off the hands of two, and threw others in the river. In another and later issue of the same journal there is a record of how a few coal porters (dock labourers) were seized by His Majesty's press-gang with the intention of compelling them to serve in the navy, and how the organised quay labourers on hearing of it, summoned their members, and marching upon the guard-house where the men were detained, attacked it, defeated the guard and released their comrades.

In the same paper, 3 January 1793, there is a letter from a gentlemen resident at Carrickmacross, Co. Monaghan, describing how an armed party of Defenders paraded through that town on its way to Ardee, how the army was brought out to attack them and a number were killed. On 24 January 1793, another correspondent tells how a battle took place betwen Bailieborough and Kingscourt, Co. Cavan, 'between those deluded persons styling themselves Defenders and a part of the army', when eighteen labourers were killed, five badly wounded, and thirty taken prisoners 'and lodged in Cavan gaol'. There is also on 23 July 1793, the following account of a battle at Limerick:

> Last night we hear that an express arrived from Limerick with the following intelligence — that on Saturday night a mob of 7 or 8,000 attacked that city and attempted to burn it; that the army, militia and citizens were obliged to join to repel these daring offenders, and to bring the artillery into the streets, and that after a severe and obstinate resistance the insurgents were dispersed with a loss of 140 killed and several wounded.
> Similar battles between the peasantry and the soldiery, aided by local landlords, occurred in the County Wexford.

In the Report of the Secret Committee of the House of Lords, 1793, speaking of the Defenders (who, as we have stated before, were the organised labourers striving to better their conditions by the only means open to them), it says, 'they first appeared in the County Louth', 'soon spread through the Counties of Meath, Cavan, Monaghan and parts adjacent', and 'their measures appear to have been concerned and conducted with the utmost secrecy and a degree of regularity and system not usual to people in such mean condition, and as if directed by men of a superior rank.'

All this, be it noted, was on the eve of the revolutionary struggle of 1798, and shows how the class struggles of the Irish workers formed the preparatory school for the insurrectionary effort.

The long drawn out struggle of the fight against tithes and the militant spirit of the Irish trades and Ribbonmen we have already spoken of as providing the revolutionary material for 1848, which Smith O'Brien and his followers were unfit to use. For the next revolutionary period, that known as the Fenian Conspiracy, the same confidence of militant class feeling and revolutionary nationalism is deeply marked. Indeed, it is no wonder that the real nationalists of Ireland, the Separatists, have always been men of broad human sympathies and intense democracy, for it has ever been in the heart of the working class at home they found their most loyal support, and in the working class abroad their most resolute defenders.

The Fenian Brotherhood was established in 1857, according to the statement of Mr John O'Mahoney, one of its two chiefs, James Stephens being the other. Of O'Mahony Mr John O'Leary says, in his **Recollections of Fenians and Fenianism**, that he was an advanced democrat of socialistic opinions, and W A O'Connor, in his **History of the Irish People**, declares that both O'Mahony and Stephens had entered into the secret societies of France, O'Mahony 'from mere sympathy'.

A further confirmation of this view of the character of the men responsible for the Fenian Society is found in a passage in a journal established in the interests of Fenianism, and published in London after the suppression of the organ of the Brotherhood, the **Irish People**, in Dublin, in 1865. This journal, the **Flag of Ireland**, quoting from the Paris correspondent of the **Irishman**, says on 3 October 1868:

> It took its rise in the Latin Quarter of this city when John O'Mahony, Michael Doheny, and James Stephens were here in exile after '48.
>
> This was the triumvirate from whose plotting brains the idea of Fenianism sprung. O'Mahony, deep in lore of Ireland and loving her traditions, found its name for the new society; Doheny, with his dogged, acute and vigorous character,

stamped it with much of the force that helped it into life, but to Stephens is due the direction it took in line of sympathy with the movements of the revolution on the Continent. He saw that the Irish question was no longer a question of religion; his common sense was too large to permit him to consider it a question of race even; he felt it was the old struggle which agitated France at the end of the last century, transferred to new ground; the opposing forces were the same, with this difference, that in Ireland the people had not the consolation in all cases of saluting tyrants as their countrymen.

The circumstance that the general chosen by Stephens to be the Commander-in-chief of the Irish Republican Army was not less a character than General Cluseret, afterwards Commander-in-chief of the Federals during the Commune of Paris, says more for the principles of the men who were the brains of the Fenian movement than any testimony of subordinates.

Coincident with the inception of Fenianism, 1857, commenced in Ireland a determined labour agitation which culminated in a vigorous movement amongst the baker journeymen against night labour and in favour of a reduction of the working hours. Great meetings were held all over the country during the years 1858-60, and in which the rights of labour were most vehemently asserted and the tyranny of the Irish employers exposed and denounced. In Wexford, Kilkenny, Clonmel and Waterford night-work was abolished and day labour established.

The movement was considered so serious that a Parliamentary Committee sat to investigate it; from its report, as quoted by Karl Marx in his great work on **Capital**, we take the following excerpts:

> In Limerick, where the grievances of the journeymen are demonstrated to be excessive, the movement has been defeated by the opposition of the master bakers, the miller bakers being the greatest opponents. The example of Limerick led to a retrogression in Ennis and Tipperary. In Cork, *where the strongest possible demonstration of feeling took place*, the masters by exercising their power of turning men out of employment, have defeated the movement. In *Dublin, the master bakers have offered*

> *the most determined opposition* to the movement, and by discountenancing as much as possible the jouneymen promoting it, have succeeded in leading the men into acquiescence in Sunday work and night work, contrary to the convictions of the men.
>
> The committee believe that the hours of labour are limited by natural laws which cannot be violated with impunity. That for master bakers to induce their workmen by the fear of losing employment, to violate their religious convictions and their better feelings, to disobey the laws of the land, and to disregard public opinion, is calculated to provoke ill-feeling between workmen and masters — and affords an example dangerous to religion, morality *and social order*.
>
> The committee believe that any constant work beyond twelve hours a day encroaches on the domestic and private life of the working man, and so leads to disastrous moral results, interfering with each man's home, and the discharge of his family's duties as a son, a brother, a husband, a father. That work beyond twelve hours has a tendency to undermine the health of the working man, and so leads to premature old age and death, to the great injury of families of working men thus deprived of the care and support of the head of the family when most required.

The reader will observe that the cities where this movement was strongest, where the workers had made the strongest fight and class feeling was highest were the places where Fenianism developed the most; it is a matter of historical record that Dublin, Cork, Wexford, Clonmel, Kilkenny, Waterford and Ennis and their respective counties were the most responsive to the message of Fenianism.

Richard Pigott, who, before he succumbed to the influence of the gold offered by the London **Times**, had a long and useful career as responsible figurehead for advanced journals in Ireland, and who in that capacity acquired a thorough knowledge of the men and movements for whom he was sponsor, gives in his **Recollections of an Irish Journalist**, this testimony as to the *personnel* of Fenianism, a testimony, it will be observed, fully bearing out our analysis of the relation between the revolutionary movement and the working class:

It is notorious that Fenianism was regarded with unconcealed aversion, not to say deadly hatred, by not merely the landlords and the ruling class, but by the Catholic clergy, the middle class Catholics, and the great majority of the farming classes. *It was in fact only amongst the youngest and most intelligent of the labouring class, of the young men of the large towns and cities engaged in the humbler walks of mercantile life, of the artisan and working classes that it found favour.*

Karl Marx qutes from 'Reports of the Poor Law Inspectors on the Wages of Agricultural Labourers in Dublin, 1870', to show that between the years 1849 and 1869, while wages in Ireland had risen fifty or sixty per cent, the prices of all necessaries had more than doubled. He gives the following extract from the official accounts of an Irish workhouse:

Average Weekly Cost Per Head

Year Ended	Provisions and Necessaries	Clothing	Total
29 Sept 1849	1s. 3¼d.	3d.	1s. 6¼d.
29 Sept 1869	2s. 7¼d.	6d.	3s. 1¼d.

The facts demonstrate that in the period during which the Fenian movement obtained its hold upon the Irish masses in the cities the workers were engaged in fierce struggles with their employers, and the price of all necessaries of life had increased twofold — two causes sufficient to cause revolutionary ferment even in a country without the historical justification for revolution possessed by Ireland.

Great Britain was also in the throes of a fierce agitation as a result of the terrible suffering of the working class resultant from the industrial crisis of 1866-7. The **Morning Star**, a London paper, stated that in six districts of London 15,000 workmen were in a state of destitution with their families; **Reynolds' Newspaper**, on 20 January 1867, quoted from a large poster, which it says was placarded all over London, the words 'Fat Oxen, Starving Men — the fat oxen from their palaces of glass have gone to feed the rich in their luxurious abode, while the starving poor are left to rot and die in their wretched dens,' and commented that 'this reminds me of the secret revolutionary associations which prepared the French people for the events of 1789. At this moment, while English workmen with their wives and children are dying of cold and hunger, there are millions of English gold — the produce of English labour — being invested in Russian, Spanish, Italian and other foreign enterprises.'

And the London **Standard** of 5 April 1866, stated: 'A frightful spectacle was to be seen yesterday in one part of the metropolis. Although the unemployed thousands of the East End did not parade with their black flags *en masse* the human torrent was imposing enough. Let us remember what these people suffer. They are dying of hunger. That is the simple and terrible fact. There are 40,000 of them. In our presence, in one quarter of this wonderful metropolis, are packed — next door to the most enormous accumulation of wealth the world ever saw — cheek by jowl with this are 40,000 helpless, starving people. These thousands are now breaking in upon the other quarters.'

This state of hunger and revolt in Great Britain offers an explanation of the curious phenomenon mentioned by A M Sullivan in **New Ireland**, that the Home Rule or constutitional journals held their own easily in Ireland itself against the **Irish People**, but in Great Britain the Fenian journal simply swept the field clear of its Irish competitors. The Irish working class exiles in Great Britain saw that the nationalist aspirations of their race pointed to the same conclusion, called for the same action, as the material interests of their class — viz. the complete overthrow of the capitalist government and the national and social tyranny upon which it rested.

Any thoughtful reader of the poems of J F O'Connell — such, for instance, as 'An Artisan's Garret', depicting in words that burn the state of mind of an unemployed Fenian artisan of Dublin beside the bedside of his wife dying of hunger — or the sweetly pleading poetry of J K Casey (Leo), cannot wonder at the warm reception journals containing such teaching met in Great Britain amidst the men and women of Irish race and of a subject class.

Just as '98 was an Irish expression of the tendencies embodied in the First French Revolution, as '48 throbbed in sympathy with the democratic and social upheavals on the Continent of Europe and England, so Fenianism was a responsive throb in the Irish heart to those pulsations in the heart of the European working class which elsewhere produced the International Working Men's Association. Branches of that association flourished in Dublin and Cork until after the Paris Commune, and it is an interesting study to trade the analogy between the course of development of the socialist movement of Europe after the Commune and that of the Irish revolutionary cause after the failure of '67. In both cases we witness the abandonment of insurrection and the initiation of a struggle in which the revolting class, while aiming at revolution, consistently refuse the arbitrament of an armed struggle.

When the revolutionary nationalists threw in their lot with the Irish Land League, and made the land struggle the basis of their warfare, they were not only placing themselves in touch once more with those inexhaustible quarries of material interests from which all the great Irish statesmen from St Laurence O'Toole to Wolfe Tone drew the stones upon which they built their edifice of a militant patriotic Irish organisation, but they were also, consciously or unconsciously, placing themselves in accord with the principles which underlie and inspire the modern movement of labour. This fact was recognised at the time by most dispassionate onlookers. Thus in a rather amusing book published in France in 1887, under the title of **Chez Paddy**, Englished as **Paddy at Home**, the author, a French aristocrat, Baron E de Mandat-Grancey, giving an account of a tour in Ireland in 1886, in the course of which he made the acquaintance of many of the Land League leaders, as well as visited at the mansions of a number of the landlords, makes this comment:

> For in fact, however they may try to dissimulate it, the Irish claims, if they do not yet amount to Communism as their avowed object — and they may still retain a few illusions upon that point — still it is quite certain that the methods employed by the Land League would not be disowned by the most advanced Communists.

It was a recognition of this fact which induced the **Irish World**, the chief advocate of the Land League in America, to carry the sub-title of 'American Industrial Liberator', and to be the mouthpiece of the nascent labour movement of those days, as it was also a recognition of this fact which prompted the Irish middle class leaders to abandon the land fight, and to lend their energies to an attempt to focus the whole interest of Ireland upon a parliamentary struggle as soon as ever a temporary set-back gave them an opportunity to counsel a change of tactics.

They feared to call into existence a spirit of enquiry into the right of property which would not halt at a negation of the sacredness of fortunes founded upon rent, but might also challenge the rightfulness of fortunes drawn from profit and interest. They instinctively realised that such an inquiry would reveal that there was no fundamental difference between such fortunes; that they were made, not from land in the one case nor workshops in the other, but from the social subjection of the non-possessing class, compelled to toil as tenants on the land or as employees in workshop or factory.

For the same reason the Land League (which was founded in 1879 at Irishtown, Co. Mayo, at a meeting held to denounce the exactions of a certain priest in his capacity as a rackrenting landlord) had had at the outset to make headway in Ireland against the opposition of all the official Home Rule press, and in Great Britain amongst the Irish exiles to depend entirely upon the championship of poor labourers and English and Scottish socialists. In fact, those latter were, for years, the principal exponents and interpreters of Land League principles to the British masses, and they performed their task unflinchingly at a time when the 'respectable' moneyed men of the Irish communities in Great Britain cowered in dread of the displeasure of their wealthy British neighbours.

Afterwards, when the rising tide of victorious revolt in Ireland compelled the Liberal Party to give a half-hearted acquiescence to the demands of the Irish peasantry, and the Home Rule-Liberal alliance was consummated, the Irish businessmen in Great Britain came to the front and succeeded in worming themselves into all the places of trust and leadership in Irish organisations.

One of the first and most bitter fruits of that alliance was the use of the Irish vote against the candidates of the Socialist and Labour

Parties. Despite the horrified and energetic protests of such men as Michael Davitt, the solid phalanx of Irish voters was again and again hurled against the men who had fought and endured suffering, ostracism and abuse for Ireland at a time when the Liberal government was packing Irish jails with unconvicted Irish men and women.

In so manoeuvring to wean the Irish masses in Great Britain away from their old friends, the Socialist and Labour Clubs, and to throw them into the arms of their old enemies, the Liberal capitalists, the Irish bourgeois politicians were very astutely following their class interests, even while they cloaked their action under the name of patriotism. Obviously a union of Irish patriotism and socialist activity, if furthered and endorsed by Irish organisations in Great Britain, could not long be kept out of, or if introduced could not well be fought, in Ireland. Hence their frantic and illogical endeavour to twist and distort the significance of Irish history, and to put the question of property, its ownership and development, out of order in all discussions on Irish nationality.

But that question so dreaded rises again; it will not lie down, and cannot be suppressed. The partial success of the Land League has effected a change in Ireland, the portent of which but few realise. Stated briefly, it means that the recent Land Acts, acting contemporaneously with the development of trans-Atlantic traffic, are converting Ireland from a country governed according to the conception of feudalism into a country shaping itself after capitalistic laws of trade.

Today the competition of the trust-owned farms of the United States and the Argentine Republic is a more deadly enemy to the Irish agriculturalist than the lingering remnants of landlordism or the bureaucratic officialism of the British Empire. Capitalism is now the enemy, it reaches across the ocean; and after the Irish agriculturalist has gathered his harvest and brought it to market he finds that a competitor living three thousand miles away under a friendly flag has undersold him and beggared him.

The merely political heresy under which class *doctrinaires* have for nearly 250 years cloaked the Irish fight for freedom has thus run its course. The fight made by the Irish septs against the English Pale and all it stood for, the struggle of the peasants, the labourers of the

18th and 19th centuries, the great social struggle of all the ages will again rise and re-shape itself in Ireland to suit the new conditions. That war which the Land League fought, and then abandoned, before it was either lost or won, will be taken up by the Irish toilers on a broader field with sharper weapons, and a more comprehensive knowledge of all the essentials of permanent victory.

As the Irish septs of the past were accounted Irish or English according as they rejected or accepted the native or foreign social order, as they measured their oppression or freedom by their loss or recovery of the collective ownership of their lands, so the Irish toilers from hence forward will base their right for freedom not upon the winning or losing the right to talk in an Irish parliament, but upon their progress towards the mastery of those factories, workshops and farms upon which a people's bread and liberties depend.

As we have again and again pointed out, the Irish question is a social question. The whole age-long fight of the Irish people against their oppressors resolves itself in the last analysis into a fight for the mastery of the means of life, the sources of production, in Ireland. Who would own and control the land? The people, or the invaders; and if the invaders, which set of them — the most recent swarm of land thieves, or the sons of the thieves of a former generation?

These were the bottom questions of Irish politics, and all other questions were valued or deprecated in the proportion to which they contributed to serve the interests of some of the factions who had already taken their stand in this fight around property interests.

Without this key to the meaning of events, this clue to unravel the actions of 'great men', Irish history is but a welter of unrelated facts, a hopeless chaos of sporadic outbreaks, treacheries, intrigues, massacres, murders, and purposeless warfare. With this key all things become understandable and traceable to their primary origin; without this key the lost opportunities of Ireland seem such as to bring a blush to the cheek of the Irish worker; with this key Irish history is a lamp to his feet in the stormy paths of today.

Yet plain as this is to us today, it is undeniable that for two hundred years at least all Irish political movements ignored this fact, and were conducted by men who did not look below the political surface. These men to arouse the passions of the people invoked the memory of social wrongs, such as evictions and famines, but for these wrongs proposed only political remedies, such as changes in taxation or transference of the seat of government (class rule) from one country to another. Hence they accomplished nothing, because the political remedies proposed were unrelated to the social subjection at the root of the matter.

The revolutionists of the past were wiser, the Irish socialists are wiser today. In their movement the North and South will again clasp hands, again will it be demonstrated, as in '98, that the pressure of a common exploitation can make enthusiastic rebels out of a Protestant working class; earnest champions of civil and religious liberty out of Catholics, and out of both a united social democracy.

SUGGESTED READING

OTHER WRITINGS BY James Connolly are not easy to come by. Much of what he wrote appeared as articles in papers such as **The Workers' Republic**. The following pamphlets give some idea of the breadth of his political ideas: **Erin's Hope and the New Evangel, The Reconquest of Ireland, Workshop Talks** and **Labour, Nationality and Religion**. These are published by the Irish Communist Party. Further selections, though these may be out of print, are available in Edwards and Ransome, **James Connolly: Selected Political Writings** (London 1973) and **James Connolly: Selected Writings**, edited by Peter Beresford-Ellis (Harmondsworth, 1973).

There are two major biographies of Connolly, C Desmond Greaves, **The Life and Times of James Connolly** (London 1976) and Samuel Levinson, **James Connolly: A Biography** (London 1973). Of these, Greaves is the more comprehensive, but is marred by his Stalinist politics. In addition to these, two recent studies are useful: Bernard Ransome, **Connolly's Marxism** (London 1980) is written in a dense, academic style but makes some useful points; also helpful is Sean Cronin, **Young Connolly** (Dublin 1978). The Irish Workers' Party have also produced a collection of articles titled **Lenin: The Irish Question** (Dublin, no date), which carries Lenin's comments on the Home Rule crisis, the 1913 lock-out and the 1916 Rising.

Finally, readers who want to take **Labour in Irish History** further could do much worse than read Emile Strauss, **Irish Nationalism and British Democracy** (London 1951) and Arthur Mitchell, **Labour in Irish Politics 1890-1930** (Dublin 1974).

ALSO FROM BOOKMARKS

Ireland's Permanent Revolution
by Chris Bambery
For 300 years it has been 'the Irish problem'. Labour and Tory, reformists and hard-liners, the soft hand of parliament and the mailed fist of the army — all have failed to solve it. This book argues for a socialist solution. £1.95 / US$4.75

The Revolutionary Road to Socialism
by Alex Callinicos
Which way for socialism today, with right-wing governments in the ascendant in the majority of the developed world? This short book puts the case for revolutionary socialism, taking up the issues of why capitalism is in the grip of economic crisis, why reformist parties have failed to protect the working class, and what went wrong after the great achievement of the Russian Revolution of 1917. £1.95 / US$3.50

Festival of the Oppressed
Solidarity, Reform and Revolution in Poland 1980-81
by Colin Barker
On 13 December 1981 the Polish military moved in to suppress the independent trade union Solidarity. It had existed less than 16 months — but during that brief time it had proved itself one of the most impressive working-class movements the world had seen in well over half a century. Solidarity vividly and dramatically revealed the possibilities open to an advanced working class when once it challenges the structures of domination in modern society.
£4.25 / US$8.50